INVISIBLE SCAR TISSUE I

Break Through Your Spiritual Scars and Reclaim Your Victory Story

Charles Anthony Solorio

Invisible Scar Tissue I: Break Through Your Spiritual
Scars and Reclaim Your Victory Story
Copyright © 2026 by Charles Anthony Solorio
Cover design by Patrick Knowles

This is a work of non-fiction. The publisher and the author have made every effort to ensure that the information in this book was correct at press time. And while this publication is designed to provide accurate information regarding the subject matter covered, the publisher and the author assume no responsibility for errors, inaccuracies, omissions, or any other inconsistencies herein, and hereby disclaim any liability to any party for any loss, damage, or disruption caused by errors or omissions, whether such errors or omissions result from negligence, accident, or any other cause.

This work has been independently timestamped by True Origin™ to document authorship and date of existence. Official timestamp documentation is available from the publisher.

Printed in the United States of America

Hardcover ISBN: 978-1-965253-96-0
Paperback ISBN: 978-1-965253-97-7
Ebook ISBN: 978-1-965253-98-4

Acknowledgments

I give thanks to You, Lord. You guided many to guide me through all my years, and You connected all the dots I have seen. It has been a great honor and privilege to see Your Story and how I, and we, fit. Open my eyes to see what You see!

I give thanks to my wife and my adult children. You supported me in ways that you are not even aware. You have been hearing the main principles of this book off and on for decades. God used each of us to test these principles, and all your responses helped shape this book.

Thank you to all my friends, coworkers, and the pastors and teachers who taught me so much. Thank you to the readers who gave me feedback. Thank you to DartFrog publishers. Thank you to Dara, Dora, and Patrick. You are all true artists and inspirations.

Claire, you were always there for me, even when I was not there. Your sacrifices helped birth this book. I love you and I thank you.

Contents

CHAPTER 1
Did Somebody Take You Away?

I t always comes back to Story.

Your Author proclaims you are not who you think you are, and your story is not what you think it is.

And one six-year-old girl's story helped change mine forever. It influenced me to write this book.

A mother put her baby girl into her crib. She probably sang lullabies to her in Spanish and marveled at how much a mother could love a child. *Mija.* She stepped back and admired the beautiful daughter she had longed for, now finally resting in a peaceful sleep.

An adult can look into the mirror over the course of several years and see the gradual effects of the passage of time. But there are "glitches" when a parent can almost pause time and, in an unveiled moment, the same deteriorating and aging eyes in the mirror can clearly see the brevity of life while observing their growing children.

Kids can grow up seemingly overnight. Perhaps the mother gazed down at her sleeping daughter and realized she needed to memorize these daily moments before they were gone.

Hours later, everything changed. A fire engulfed her daughter's bedroom. The lifelong dream of having a daughter ended in minutes. The mother was unable to rescue her love. Her daughter was gone. The fire was so extensive and the heat so great there were no remains left.

Though her baby was gone, the mother never completely let go of the love she had for her daughter. Though her daughter and time passed, her love never did.

A few years later, the woman was at a child's birthday party, surrounded by kids, each child a reminder of how things could have been if her daughter was still alive. How many times in the last six years or so did she wonder if her daughter could have been like yet another little girl before her.

And at this party, she fixated her attention toward another random six-year-old girl who reminded her of herself and what her daughter would have looked like if she were still alive.

Her hair would have probably been the same color and length. Those eyes. Those deeper-shade-of-brown eyes reminded her of her own mother, passed down to another generation. How tall would her daughter be now? What would her personality be like?

But something was different this time. This birthday party was different. This little girl before her was different from any other six-year-old girl she had encountered before.

She is my daughter.

A mother knows these kinds of things. But how could this be? *This* six-year-old girl right in front of her? She stood out from all the other kids running wild at the party. Something awoke inside the mother. A memory of the last time she'd put her daughter down to sleep.

Though other kids at the party stopped for no one and continued running and screaming in joy, the ticking clock of life paused as the mother gazed into the eyes of the girl in front of her. All was quiet around her. Except for the woman's own voice in her head.

She is my baby.

But how could the girl in front of her be *her daughter?* Her daughter had been killed in a fire six years before. But the screaming kids at a loud birthday party could not quiet the voice in her head.

What could she possibly do if her little girl was no longer dead and was now at the party accompanied with her "parents"?

Did she rise from the dead? She could not go to the parents and say, "Your daughter is mine. I am taking her home now." Right? The woman went to the little girl in secret and told her she had gum in her hair and that she could help her take it out. The mother took a few strands of the girl's hair.

Through DNA testing, she discovered the girl was her daughter.

She later found out that someone had abducted her infant daughter and burned down the house to cover up the crime.[1]

You and Me

When I read this story several years ago, I thought I was like that little girl. I too believed someone's lie, which influenced me to believe I was somebody other than who I was meant to be. I lived somebody else's lie. I believed in a coming death sentence. This lie changed my life.

I sometimes still struggle with my old false identities and fear of death today. I have come to believe that, to varying degrees, *you* are also like this little girl. To varying degrees, we have each believed lies about who we are.

Have we, in a sense, been taken away from our true home and groomed to live a lie apart from who we really are? As we wander and drift away from our true Story, are we living in the fullness of liberty and strength? In our relationships, do we freely move and grow in full faith and confidence? Or are we stuck in broken ways, entangled in the webwork of invisible scars from old physical and spiritual injuries, weakened by our beliefs that we are who someone else has defined us to be?

---

[1] Christine Pelisek, "Mom Thought Her Baby Was Killed in House Fire. But She'd Really Been Kidnapped and Was Living 15 Miles Away," *People*, November 17, 2024.

Deception is the most powerful tool used against us. How often do you and I know in the moment that we are deceived? What lies are you and I living without even knowing we are living a lie? Can we get back to who we really are?

This is at the heart of what we will explore in this series.

A Little About My Backstory

A life-changing death in my family "abducted" me and rooted deep within me, influencing what I believed to be my identity and fate (more on that later). Unseen wounds and injuries locked me and restricted me within myself, like an internal mobile and invisible prison.

I grew up wanting to participate in the healing of others as well as my own. I became a physical therapist to literally get my hands on what ailed fellow wounded travelers in life. Along the way, I learned how our physical challenges are interrelated with our internal spiritual victories and losses.

I also learned about story structure and started a fictional series moving from the beginning of time and through the eras of slavery, the *Mayflower*, and the Revolutionary War. I hope to take that story from the past to our present and into our hope in a full-of-light future.

The story of the mother and her abducted daughter illustrates how the system we live in attempts to abduct us away from home and attempts to define, identify, and groom us to place our trust in untrustworthy sources.

But Someone refuses to believe the lie of your death. Someone refuses to believe you have no more remains. Someone has not given up on you and draws you closer to tell you who you really are and to reveal your Story—the one you are not aware of.

Spiritual Injuries Invite a Spiritual Question

We each have our individual painful stories. We have our mental/emotional/spirit and physical injuries. We have our wounds. Our injuries and wounds limit and restrict how we move. We each desire to move with more spiritual freedom of movement, strength, and power in our lives.

Can the principles of physical rehabilitation and Story break through our spiritual scar tissue?

I will share with you what I have learned in my career in physical rehabilitation and Story and how this transformed me and allows me to navigate and move in new freedom and strength in a new identity—and how this can change you.

I Am Confronting a Story of Atrophy and Paralysis

We can lose our normal and healthy movement and strength in life. We can get spiritual atrophy and paralysis too.

This is not a self-improvement book. I will actually present the case for the exact opposite. Stop beating yourself and others up because you cannot self-improve with only your limited vision and willpower. We will see how this is the best news you have heard in a long time.

I've had patients on their first physical therapy visit tell me that I could not help them because of all their previous injuries and surgeries and long-term degenerative changes, and they were not even sure why they were there to see me, because nothing could be done. I enjoy confronting that same common narrative in our heads regarding our lives. You know it well, because I know it for myself: No one can change my past, present, or future life story with all my mistakes and the mistakes committed against me. I am who I am.

Can you change your broken story? Can you change your past?

Your past story may have parts that look broken and unfixable with your mistakes and the mistakes of others affecting you. Perhaps you have believed and adopted a name, an identity given to you. Loser. Perhaps you wonder if you will always lose in your relationships and dreams. That's just the way it has always been in your family.

But there is more to your Story.

What I Know

Perhaps you have a history of trauma and/or great pain. Or maybe you made a bad decision that changed the course of who you were. Maybe words were said over you that cut so deep. Perhaps you continued the flaws and weaknesses of addictions, fears, or anxiety from previous generations of your family.

We each, in a real sense, have scar tissue from spiritual wounds, our mental and emotional wounds, but there is an Author who desires to heal us and break through our webs of interconnecting scar tissue to free us into full freedom of movement and strength and into His unveiling narrative.

You can know more of your unlocked life to then move confidently in your newfound growing faith and into the coming difficult and joyous chapters of life.

What Your Physical Rehabilitation
Storyteller Has to Offer

I have two passions that have directed much of my life. I have been a physical therapist treating and assessing movement and strength and function for over thirty-seven years. I estimate in the near future I will have provided close to ninety thousand patient treatments in my career.

I have also studied writing and story structure for the last twenty years. I have written three fiction books, taken a writing class, attended writing conferences, and read dozens of books and articles on writing. I have been known to ruin a good movie with family and friends by deconstructing narrative structures and raising questions.

If each person has a superpower, perhaps mine is the ability to see and connect patterns. I have a knack for connecting the dots of events from the past, present, and the future into the form of story, utilizing principles of movement and strength.

I will show you how there are pixels of the principles of physical therapy and Story (there is an Epic God Story and our little stories) when placed together that form part of a clearer picture of the lives of people. You will see the same pattern within you and in people you know.

My hope in this book series is to present a unique perspective pointing to a unique solution with a fresh blending of revelatory, entertaining, visionary, emotional, and cerebral ideas in a way that you have never seen before.

What's in the Coming Pages

I will share with you four of the most important questions we can ever ask and answer, which should point us toward destroying mediocrity in life. You will learn a spiritual movement and strength analysis to help you break free. You will use a medical progress note format to navigate and move toward your own healing. I will show you how your Author wants to free you as He utilizes the components of story in a way to understand and move in strength in this challenging, difficult, and wondrous world.

Somebody Wants You

Someone is seeking you, even courting you, when others, including yourself, have thought that who you hoped to be was long dead years ago. But there is something special in your DNA. An identifying marker that reveals a message.

Come join this wounded physical therapist in the wild adventure of navigating through a wonderful and dying world with a history of a broken story as we together utilize principles of physical rehabilitation and Story.

This book is for anyone stuck with a broken story and who may be lacking movement and strength for what you were created to do. It is time to break through the invisible scar tissue and move freely through an unveiled, brand-new Epic for the first time.

There is a future revolutionary transformation for you. You will never be the same.

Leave the spiritual atrophy and paralysis behind and walk into life-story rehab.

Become who He says you are, for the first time.

Prayer

Take some time and converse with God about Him and you. If you want help with specific words, you can use the following:

Lord God,

Who are You? Who am I? I am tired of being stuck where I am. Unlock me. Free me up. Remove any barriers to hearing You above all others. Soften and sensitize my heart. I want something new, and I want to try what You want. Have Your way with me. Show me You, and show me who I am in You.

Amen.

Questions

- Who are you?
- Are you living out who you are supposed to be? How?
- What false names and beliefs have you believed for yourself?
- You have had physical injuries. Do you think you have had injuries to your spirit? Share what those may be.
- How do you feel about the possibility that, despite the reports of your early death of who you were supposed to be, Someone wants you and is courting you?

CHAPTER 2

The Fear of Death and the Accompanying Scar Tissue

In 1966 my cousin Clive Junior, at eighteen years of age, decided he would fight for the country he loved in the Vietnam War. His home of Morenci, Arizona (my hometown), produced a hardy stock of young men that military recruiters longed for. The Morenci boys and their families, most Native American, Mexican American, and Caucasian, were segregated into different parts of town. But in school and in their personal lives, they did not have the contemporary racial divides of our day and were united in their love of their United States. They were good hunters in the nearby hills. There wasn't much room for pacifism in Morenci in those days.

Clive Junior became a marine. According to old family reports while I was growing up, and consistent with Kyle Longley's book *The Morenci Marines: A Tale of Small Town America and the Vietnam War*, Clive Junior became an elite Ranger who was eventually selected to be a guard for President Johnson on a visit to Guam. He became a sergeant at the age of twenty-one and led his men, literally led his men on their missions with the increased vulnerability that came with that decision, and he lost his life when an explosive device went off while on patrol in Vietnam in 1969.

My mom was devastated at losing her nephew. Clive Junior's family even more so. There was a heaviness and sense of loss that was new to me as a seven-year-old. It was the first time I remember experiencing the invading occupier of death. The sadness for my immediate and extended family is still felt today all these years later. It eases at times but never fully goes away. Some family members never fully recovered, and despair hovered over their lives until their last days.

Shortly after Clive Junior's death, I remember his remains in the casket in the front of the church memorial service in Morenci. Though I do not think of myself as an ultra-empathetic person, I know what I felt during that service. I have never been in a building with such a heavy weight of so much sadness.

I never second-guessed anyone's decision allowing me to attend at a young age. I needed to be present. As I grew older, I knew that something good would eventually come from me being there. But if I can be honest with you, this melancholy and sometimes lonely kid left that church on that day accompanied with a new, uninvited guest within me.

Death.

The fear of death.

Something entered and rooted deep inside me during the service and for the rest of my life. It influenced me in ways that only recently can I now partially see and understand.

It started with a visceral fear that I would die soon.

Years after the church service, the fear morphed. I grew up with the radio playing top-forty music (seventies and eighties were the best!) and the radio and TV news proclaiming the local and international concerns every day. In those days the reporting told us we should be concerned and prepared for a nuclear war with Russia at any moment.

Some things remain the same.

Those concerning days hit me on a visceral level. Do you have a deep-rooted fear of something that you just can't explain or completely shake? I was afraid that the country I loved would draft me for the next war and that I would die at an early age before I could live my dreams.

At the minimum, I would have to say goodbye to my family and friends and the rest of my short-term dreams and life. I wanted to be the first Mexican to play in the NBA for my favorite Lakers. How could they win another championship if I could no longer play basketball because of a war injury or if I was dead from the next war?

I lived with the soundtrack of war, or coming war, in the background of my life. I carefully paid attention, over the next several years after my cousin's death, as debates continued about whether our country would reinstate the draft. This sometimes kept me awake at night.

The depth of my fear was irrational and in some ways made no logical sense. But how often does a gripping fear make logical sense? It still rooted in me, grew, and lurked within me like a scary and somber song in the soundtrack of a horror movie. It was at times so subtle and in the background that I just acclimated to it without fully realizing it existed. I could never fully exorcise it.

I was going to die in a war in another land. It affected me in ways I could not discern until much later in life. Something downloaded into me without any obvious consent on my part. My default internal program spread pessimism. In most situations I assumed and expected the worst-possible outcome. After all, I was going to die at an early age . . . like my cousin . . . in a war. I had difficulty fully imagining a long-term future. I did not dream of marrying and having a family.

Kind of like a glass always half-empty and laced with cyanide that I would someday soon have to drink. What a miserable outlook.

When dying in a war did not happen in my teens, it then morphed from dying on a foreign battlefield to just dying. Over the years, when *any* bodily or mental issue arose, I convinced myself that I had things—heart disease, multiple sclerosis, cancer, a permanent back injury, or any other ailment—that would slowly kill what I thought my life was supposed to be and that would end my career as a physical therapist.

I had no awareness or idea how to shake the fear of death. It fought a stealthy special ops mission within me that extracted any great hope I had. There was a great war in this life, and I was going to hopelessly die fighting and losing in it.

It was like someone edited out my past and present story and convinced me to live someone else's script for me.

It was like someone made up a new name and identity from the one I was born with and took me away from the home where I once dreamed.

In hindsight, I wonder if that influenced my childhood interest in the Civil War, slavery, war in general, injuries and wounds, healing, and how we view ourselves. I was never drafted. But I did enter into the healthcare field to treat wounds from this life that is at times a battle and war. I wanted to help people heal and to help free people from pain, impaired function, and fear and anxiety accompanying the injury, and to be free to move their injured and broken body in newfound strength.

I am not a psychologist or mental health professional, but I know enough to know we are not robots. We have feelings, concerns, anxiety, and fears that are connected to our physical ailments, and some of those I treat indirectly as a physical therapist. I saw connections between mental and physical health, and I saw mental health improve with improvements in physical health.

Yet the fear of death, in its various cloaked forms, still pulled and controlled my leash.

The PT Point of View During the First Visit

Let me share what I see in a day as a physical therapist (PT). The first visit with a patient is what we call an "initial evaluation." One of our awesome physical therapy aides has usually already brought my new patient into a private room.

There is so much that occurs in the first few seconds of entering into the room for the first time to meet a patient. Back in the day when there were not too many dark-skinned PTs like me, there was sometimes an awkward look of disappointment, and/or doubt, about my skill level when a patient first saw me. I learned to not make that personal.

Or sometimes I would have a patient who was African American, or of a foreign culture, with a look of doubt. I sensed that they wondered if I was going to treat them fairly or that perhaps I might have prejudices against them. Fortunately, at least where I live, there is much diversity in people, so these awkward scenarios are a lot less frequent nowadays.

Most of the time my patient and I click within the first few minutes and the preliminary obstacles are pushed aside. Sometimes patients have had such a bad previous experience with healthcare that it can take longer. Every once in a while, our personalities just don't click, and that is okay. I then try to help them link up with someone else they can be comfortable with.

Sometimes the internal world of fears and pain spills over into the external world with crying. Any PT who has been doing physical therapy for at least several years will tell you that patients crying during the evaluation, or succeeding treatments, happens now and then. And despite our industry's reputation, it is rarely because of pain from treatment. It is almost always related to the emotional and physical roller coaster of being in pain, and its ramifications, and sometimes with the relief of pain.

Mixed in with the personality dynamics in those first few minutes is sometimes something else. There is a fear or concern in many patients' eyes that has nothing to do with me or physical therapy. It is a fear of what will happen if they don't get better and how that will affect the rest of their lives, and the lives of others.

I see this on that initial visit, and sometimes with following treatments, because their pain and injury may affect their ability to function in their career, provide for their family, or continue their favorite activity, hobby, exercise, or sport.

For the younger patient and their parents, will they be able to get that dream sports scholarship if they don't get better? Or with others, will they be able to care for someone at home when the only caretaker is now injured? Will they be able to physically work both their jobs when there is a family to care for and a mortgage and bills to pay? What will happen if they lose their job, and their health benefits, when someone at home has a chronic illness or injury? Injuries and pain, along with fear of loss of function and finances, creates a powerful combination.

Sometimes their other health issues play a role, as now with their present pain and injury, they may not be able to exercise to lose that extra weight—and now health issues related to being overweight will get worse. Imagine not being able to do what you love or not being able to work and pay your bills. Scary stuff, if you ask me.

Fortunately, I would estimate that about 85 to 90 percent of the patients I see get better and often are able to eliminate all or most of their symptoms and loss of function. But there will always be a percentage who need surgery or something else I cannot help them with. Perhaps the injury was so extensive, or a joint was too damaged, along with excessive scar tissue, and we were not able to get full range of motion and function back. This smaller percentage of times, when treatment does not bring the desired effect, is always frustrating for me and my patients.

The rest of the evaluation consists of asking questions to learn about them and their condition. I then look at their posture, their range of motion, their strength and flexibility, neurological status, and how they walk, and then conduct special tests. If the patient has made it through the medical system far enough to get to orthopedic physical therapy, then they most likely have pain and limited movement, strength, and overall function.

After we finish the patient's history and initial physical testing, I then have the patient do specific therapeutic movements, and then I retest their original findings to see if the movements changed their condition.

Often hope enters the room and pushes fear to the side when patients see that after movement-analysis testing, followed by performing certain movements and exercises, improvements in pain and function are unveiled. Their eyes open in pleasant surprise, and an invisible weight is lifted off their burdened shoulders. I am a McKenzie therapist, otherwise known as mechanical diagnosis and therapy. Most times with the first visit, we find a movement that improves their condition. Sometimes it takes additional visits though.

What Is Scar Tissue?

As an orthopedic PT, I see people who, in many cases, have sustained an injury or had surgery. Surgeons and physical therapists see the negative effects of the body laying down excessive scar tissue after an injury or the trauma of surgery.

Scar tissue is a fibrous tissue consisting of cells that the body lays down to heal the trauma. Sometimes the process goes into overdrive. Sometimes, if treatment is nonexistent or too delayed, both internal and external scar tissue can become more of a problem than the original injury or surgery.

Think of any major cut on your skin and how the body uses scar tissue to heal the open wound to then close it. Now think of internal scar tissue in overdrive, which haphazardly binds down with pain and impairs movement, adheres, and significantly limits once healthy movement and range of motion and strength. An injured knee or shoulder, with varying degrees of pain, now cannot bend or straighten or raise up as it should. Surgeons can see the scar tissue during a subsequent surgery and sometimes surgically remove the visible scar tissue.

Future Physical Therapy Treatments
After the Initial Evaluation

Every succeeding visit I continue the same process of hearing the patients' recent subjective experience, and combining with my objective findings, I then put the theory of what is causing and helping the condition to the test. I prescribe exercises to address the patients' physical deficits, both in the clinic and for the patient to perform at home. Sometimes I perform specific treatment techniques to help the patient become more autonomous with their self-care. When things go according to plan, each visit is another piece of the puzzle to complete the picture of what is happening.

One pattern I usually see is a postural, or positional, issue and/or an injury or surgery that leads to the loss of normal movement, strength, and function. A postural or positional issue could include someone with neck pain and a long history of daily sleeping on their stomach with their head always turned in the same direction. Or a patient recently having a total knee replacement who cannot straighten their knee. The loss of normal movement, strength, and function then contributes to more pain that then causes an increase in loss of normal movement, strength, and function. It is a cycle that can be hard to turn off.

In the majority of cases, as the postural and positional issues are dealt with, and as the patient is freed up to move more normally, the pain improves, even to the point that the patient is better than before experiencing their pain and/or injury.

The Daily Initial Evaluation of Life

When I walk into a different part of this big treatment room we call the world—when I go for a walk, do an errand, visit a friend, go to work, or virtually explore new areas through podcasts or the news—my initial evaluation on a daily basis is similar to yours.

In the clinic, I see the effects of fear and the loss of normal and healthy movement and strength, because of physical injuries from trauma and surgery, further complicated with corresponding scar tissue. Is it possible that we can also have similar effects of fear and loss of normal and healthy movement and strength because of invisible spirit injuries and trauma, further complicated with corresponding invisible scar tissue?

I believe that just as a patient with excessive physical scar tissue struggles with pain and loss of movement, strength, and normal function, each of us can have restricting and painful invisible scar tissue after sustaining spirit injuries with corresponding pain and loss of normal movement, strength, and normal function in our relationships.

From a biblical point of view, I believe we are body, soul, and spirit. When I mention spirit, I am referring to the general population's idea of the immaterial part of us, the "spiritual" part of us.

For example, a heartbreaking betrayal from a loved one can injure a person's spirit, and the pain and memories of that injury can, in a sense, produce invisible scar tissue where that injured person may then have difficulty giving their love to another. Imagine a webwork of invisible spirit scars consisting of painful memories with fear, guilt, shame, and regret, which restrict our attempts at healthy movement.

And just like I see in the clinic with orthopedic issues and the physical consequences from injuries, we can sustain internal wounds from our various emotional injuries and become spiritually stiff, stuck, and weak in our broken ways—which limits our ability to move freely with strength or power in our stories.

When I am out and about in the waiting room of life and waiting for my name to be called, I see and hear fear and concern about personal, local, and world events in almost everyone— even with those who attempt to ignore the background-news soundtrack. I believe that you also sense that same degree of fear and concern about life around you.

You and I see, with our self-evaluations, a loss of freedom of movement and strength from previous spirit injuries. We each scar down and get stuck in our broken ways and lose the movement and strength that we perhaps once had, or always wanted to have.

How does this happen?

Our Injuries

We each, to varying degrees, make the same mistakes and succumb to the same toxic appetites that are common in each of us. I have had issues with viewing pornography in my past, but that might not be your issue. Perhaps you just can't separate yourself from your unhealthy appetite for illegal drugs, excessive alcohol, food, sexual sin, money, power, control, etcetera.

There are challenges common to all of humanity, but each vary by degrees on an individual level.

When you walk around in the waiting room, or treatment room, of life, you see what I see. Excessive stress and anxiety. Depression. Suicides. Division. Crime. Homelessness. Drug and alcohol issues. Various health issues. Words spoken that cut and twist more than any physical knife ever could. A death of a loved one, relationship, or dream. I see people in spiritual pain isolating themselves, while others heroically battle through their pain to make this a better world.

As I share these same emotions and challenges, I wonder about each person's story, and I wonder what labels or false names we each carry, as if they are our real name. Here are some possible names: Hopeless. Loser. Regret. Addict. Unfaithful. Stupid. Timid. Selfish. Fear. Death.

If we are honest with confronting the challenges of life, we should be able to perform an initial evaluation on ourselves every day. We can see the results from our tests and examinations of movement and strength in our relationships—if we dare to.

Optimally, there should not be estranged relationships with spouses, ex-spouses, children, friends, coworkers. But there is. Perhaps when we look at our lives straight on, there is a loss of healthy strength and movement accompanied with fear, which has moved into the big room and pushed hope aside.

You see all the findings from your own testing. You know something is not healthy, and it affects each person. If you had to summarize your initial evaluation of yourself, what would your diagnosis be? If we cannot find the right diagnosis to reveal the concern, it will be difficult to fix the problem with the right treatment.

How do we navigate and make sense of life as we wander in the big waiting room, dreading to be called in for testing that will find us wanting?

Same as I do with my evaluations and treatments in the clinic. With questions.

What are the most important questions we can ask and answer that can help us diagnose what we know is broken and stuck?

Prayer

Take some time and converse with God about anything. If you want help with specific words, you can use the following:

God,
Do I have any deeply rooted fears?
Where have I had injuries to my spirit?
Show me where I have unhealthy appetites.
Show me how you evaluate me and show me how You can heal me.
Amen.

Questions

- Have you ever had a deep-rooted fear that forced someone else's script on you?
- How have your fears influenced who you are today?
- How are you moving and how is your strength in your life and relationships?
- What is your initial evaluation of many around you regarding how they move and how their strength is in their relationships and lives in general?
- Considering your spirit injuries and their effects on you—have they affected how you navigate in life?

CHAPTER 3
Question Mediocrity

Is there a best way to enter into a weightier and deeper conversation that supersedes the typical superficial conversation? If you are like me, you long for a time when you and a loved one could get into a memorable conversation that then acts as a foundation to build upon or repair that particular relationship. This is greater than gold.

So with that in mind, I say this: You are not who you think you are.

Let's confront a fear head on and move toward examining your hidden self and enter into a deeper revelation of who you really are, in order to grow and mature in new and healthy ways.

What is the best way to enter into a deeper conversation with others and within yourself?

Deep and probing questions.

I ask my patients direct questions when discerning what is causing their physical pain and loss of function. At some point it is best to cut the small talk and get right to the heart of the matter. The answers to these questions will help me to help my patients. Over the years, this then helps me to help others.

The right direct questions can also help us discover the root of our pains and losses in the spiritual realm. This is where people like Greg Koukl have influenced me over the years, with his organization Stand to Reason, which trains Christians to think clearly and give a defense of their faith. He advocates using strategic questions to clarify and point toward truth.

I came up with a few questions that I now use with others, as well as with myself. Let us courageously dive in.

The Four Questions of the Apocalypse Riding upon Mediocrity

In physical therapy, and more specifically as a McKenzie PT, the heart of my subjective exam—my questions to hear the patient's evidence of their problem—comes down to four main questions, which tell me the most information in the shortest time.

- Where are your symptoms?
- How long have you had the symptoms?
- Are your symptoms constant or intermittent?
- Are your symptoms getting better, worse, or staying the same?

Though there are many other questions I ask to create a clearer picture, these four help me classify the problem into one of four main categories, or classifications, which directs me toward the appropriate treatment.

Just as I use four main questions in physical therapy to help determine the truth of a patient's condition, I believe there are four main questions to help determine the truth of a person's spiritual condition of pain, movement, and strength for their walk in life.

Those nearest me know I like to talk about deep and weighty things. Being older than some around me, I like to break through the superficial life with some challenging questions that I have wrestled with.

When asking the questions, I often let people know that they don't have to tell me their answers and that I am just presenting the questions for them to meditate on. If they want to share their answers with me, that would be great, and it *always* leads to deeper and interesting discussions. I am mainly learning more information from each person, which I build on for future conversations.

Regarding myself, I answer the questions to learn about who I am, and I return to the same four questions periodically to see in which direction I am moving. In every experience in life, it is wise for me to recalibrate back to how I am answering some, or all, of these questions.

In the book of Revelation, we read about what many know as the four horsemen of the apocalypse. These four horsemen are part of God's judgment on an evil world, to judge and turn hearts toward God before it is too late.

I call the following questions the "Four Questions of the Apocalypse Riding upon Mediocrity" or "The Four Questions," as they wreak havoc on lives of mediocrity and status quo. Lives stuck and locked. In this case, these questions are not meant to be a final judgment but an awakening to the reality of how we live our lives, to then prevent us from failing in our final judgment before the throne of God.

I sometimes ask one question at a time and allow days or weeks or months before I ask another of the questions with the same person. Other times they come in bunches, depending on what God is doing at the time. I usually ask these questions in this order, but the timing of each is always an adventure, because I do not know the pacing of the questions until I am in the midst of the conversation.

Here we go.

The Four Questions of the Apocalypse
Riding upon Mediocrity

- *Why* are you alive?
- *What* do you live for?
- *Who* do you live for?
- What is *most important* in life?

There you go. Simple. They cut. Through layers. Transformational.

If we are humble. Honest. Vulnerable.

Why Are You Alive?

A few years before my father died, he dropped a bombshell of a story on my sister.

Before he legally immigrated to the US from Mexico, my father applied for what we believe was a work visa to work in the US. This likely occurred in the 1940s. They sent word to him that he was approved and that he just had to find a way to get from his home in the southern tip of Baja California, Mexico, to the US and Mexican border.

Without a car, with having equal to a second-grade education, without knowing how to read or write, without speaking English, my father killed birds and snakes for food as he made his way up north. Closer to his destination, and after having used up all the money his mother had saved for him, he hitched a ride on a freight train.

The person he communicated with said he could board . . . on top of the train. On top of the train?! While he was up there, another man climbed on top while the train was moving. Perhaps he'd been told the same thing? He pulled out a knife and approached my father. Maybe he thought my father had money? Is it possible he was told only one person could travel on top of the train? Perhaps he was just mentally unstable or just plain evil.

He lunged at my dad, and a fight ensued on top of the moving train. They fought, though my father was unarmed. Remember, this scene occurred before any *Mission Impossible* movies.

My father paused with the telling of the story. My sister was stunned in silence. Then she blurted the most obvious question, "Well, obviously you made it, because you are here today. What happened to the man?"

My father paused, looked down. "Well . . . he fell down."

That was all the story that he was willing to share.

What does this story have to do with you?

You probably have a story or two where you could have died, and probably in ways you are not even aware of. And if you do not have a tale like that, your parents, grandparents, or previous ancestors have or had stories of how they probably should have died before you were born. If one of them would have died at a certain time, perhaps you would not have been born. We all have stories if we search far enough. Perhaps you, or a key member of your ancestors, had cancer, a heart attack, or risked their lives in the military or the police or while firefighting, etcetera.

My father probably should have died. If he had died, he would have never met who was later to be my mom. I would have never came to be. I myself have a story or two where I could have died.

So considering *your* life and previous relatives, *why* are you alive?

Take a few moments, or several minutes, to pray and think about this before you read on.

What Do You Live For?

What do you love to do? Perhaps you live to travel, to exercise, to eat a great meal, to spend time with loved ones. What great joy it is to watch somebody who is living what they love to do. Often there is a great skill exhibited. Perhaps you have seen a gifted athlete, or perhaps a gifted coach or actress, up close and personal and witnessed their special ability in action. They operate in another gear and at another level than most people in that particular arena of life.

Maybe you have such a gift.

Is it not fun to watch a roofer, carpenter, musician, or artist articulate a great truth, or a gifted teacher present a workshop, or a charismatic speaker motivate you to try harder? Though your gifting may be different, you know what I am talking about. There are, or have been, moments where you shifted into another gear within yourself that even surprised yourself. Something clicks and you almost effortlessly shift into that other gear. There may be something that other people have told you that you are really good at and you just think that anybody could do the same thing.

But *what* do you live for?

What is it that puts joy, energy, and fuel into your life tank? Fuel that gives energy for the challenges in life. It confirms internally that you were created for a purpose and gives a sense of honor to be alive to exercise that very purpose you were created for.

Creating is related to what you live for. What do you love to create? For me, it is often writing. Maybe for you it is creating memories with family and friends, a new dish to share, gardening, painting, or playing ball.

You are made in the image of the ultimate Creator, so of course you should create!

What is it that you live for?

Take some time to pray and think about this before you move to the next section.

Who Do You Live For?

It's time to be totally transparent. When you have to make important decisions for yourself, among all within your circle of influences, who ultimately has the greatest influence on casting the deciding vote in your head on any important matter?

Who ultimately do you live for?

Who do you ultimately aim to please?

Take a few minutes with God and seek the truth.

What Is Most Important in Life?

How much of your time, energy, and money are spent on maintaining, or changing, your image before others, to gain more money and material things, power and control, to have more sex, more prestige from your job? Self-awareness, money, material things, sex, and work can all be healthy and normal things, but they can become toxic when we are out of whack with our appetites and desires.

How many times have you had a crazy dread about an issue in your life? Perhaps there is an issue with a family member, friend, or coworker. Think of all the time and energy we spend on our fears, and for what purpose?

But what is most important?

In my teens when I struggled with the belief that I would die soon, I tried to use what I called the "deathbed test." Imagine you are living in a future day and you are dying. Lying in bed and staring up at the ceiling or out the window, you have had plenty of time to reflect on your life. Perhaps you have had struggles with some of the things mentioned in the previous paragraphs. Or maybe you had little to none of the above. In your final hours, if you are able to think clearly, what is now most important?

What is most important in life?

Take a few minutes and pray on that.

To get our answers, we need to take a deep breath, exhale, and take a closer look in the mirror.

Prayer

Take time to converse with God. You can choose the following words if that helps.

> *Lord,*
>
> *I believe there is great purpose and design with everything You do. I believe You made me with Your great design and for a great purpose. Soften my heart, and open my ears and my eyes to experience You. Show me more of You, and show me who I am in You. Show me what is most important.*
>
> *Amen.*

Questions

- Why are you alive?
- What do you live for?
- Who do you live for?
- What is most important in life?

CHAPTER 4
It's Not About You

Just as a medical practitioner utilizes a subjective examination with probing questions to help learn the truth of a patient's condition, so we have utilized questions in the previous chapter to help us discern more truth of our inner condition.

You and I answered the four questions of the why, who, and what to learn more about ourselves. Were you honest and transparent with yourself? What did you learn? Perhaps your internal eyes of self-examination revealed the same thing I learned about myself.

Yup. I am taking a deep breath after using a virtual mirror to reflect what and who I see.

This is what I found out. If I am honest . . . it is all about me. The following is my ugly truth.

Why am I alive? I am alive because I am supposed to live for what makes me happy and feel fulfilled. At times I may vocalize or convince myself that I live for others, but in most instances when I present my image before others and I have rationalized and justified all my desires, my thoughts and actions demonstrate I ultimately live for me.

Ouch.

What do I live for? I live to make myself happy. I live to make myself more confident, secure, and significant, to make people like me more, for more respect, all in my own eyes as well as through the eyes of others. I want people to like me and to think I am great and really important.

Who do I live for? I live for me, and then after that I live to make myself feel better by helping others. If I objectively look at my thoughts, my money accounts, my time with my screens, my calendar, and my intentions, where does my most valuable time, energy, and money go toward? Most of the time . . . yup. Eventually for me.

What is most important in life? Most of the times this answer fluctuates according to my circumstances and whims. When I am more level headed and in a good place emotionally, when I fluctuate toward my best, my love for me and then for others fuels my happiness and importance.

The scary truth is, I am not the only one with tendencies toward these self-centered answers.

And perhaps because I think our culture actually grooms us to think this way, I can begin to think that this is actually "normal" because everybody else in my favorite movies and TV shows, as well as those around me, is the same way to varying degrees!

Homework

You probably know I give each of my patients homework, which I assign to help them get better each day. It usually consists of postural and positional awareness and specific exercises designed to address the deficits found on their examination and sessions.

I have some homework for you that will just take a few minutes and possibly change how you look at things. Look up the live performance video or just listen to the song "If We're Honest" by Francesca Battistelli and then look up the lyrics.

All done? Can a song be drop-dead gorgeous? This song is drop-dead gorgeous. Powerful lyrics all the way through. Sincere and authentic singing. It can cut through some layers of our multilayered masks. All the words are powerful, but I want you to take a look at that first line again. Think about it.

Brutal. Cold. Hard truth. But truth that costs can liberate our movement and strength. Our subjective evaluation of ourselves with the four questions is brutal, if we're honest. The four questions can help us get there. Don't be too hard on yourself, because this is just a snapshot of where you and I are in this season. Hope is coming!

Exposed

We live for ourselves.

Hopefully, the Four Questions of the Apocalypse provided judgment and illumination upon our mediocrity and status quo. But we are more than our limitations. Placing ourselves at the center of the universe through our eyes above all others limits how we see things.

Am I all there really is in life? Are you all there is?

I am convinced that many of the famous celebrities who ended up addicted to drugs, sex, money, power, and committed suicide (and some even now committing gradual suicide) were stuck in the small view of life. How distressing it would be to seek fame, money, sex, power, and control over our lives, to then experience some of the fruits of our quest, and then discover it was a trap, with each of us locked inside miserable, self-centered, and self-deceived.

How depressing to find out I lived with every possible purpose in my self-serving life to scale the tallest mountain and then collapse at the peak of the small mound of dirt, with lost time I can never regain and the realization that I was king of a small, selfish life. I don't know about you, but I can understand how one could then question if life was worth living anymore.

Before we point our finger at another powerful and influential famous person in rehab or after another gradual suicide progression, we should remember that is where each of us will be if our lives are left unchecked with our ultimate base desires.

So is there more to life than what we currently live? Is there something bigger than us? Is there something greater than just our desires and appetites?

We are swimming toward deeper and loftier thinking waters. Take the dive with me and let us see that the swimming hole we jumped into is actually an ocean connected to all other oceans.

My Studies

In my research over the years, I have found the evidence for the existence of God to be quite overwhelming. I would even say, in hindsight, that much of it is self-evident. Researching the evidence and then recognizing and accepting what should be a self-evident truth are two very different things. It all comes down to whether one *wants* to see, acknowledge, and then accept the evidence. It will be difficult to see and acknowledge what one does not want to see and acknowledge.

You can read some of the fantastic works from the influencers of my internal and external discussions over the years, like Josh McDowell, Norman Geisler, Hugh Ross, Henry Morris, William Lane Craig, Gary Habermas, J. P. Moreland, Peter Kreeft, Greg Koukl, Fred Heeren, Lee Strobel, Phillip Johnson, Ravi Zacharias, Michael Behe, all my former and present pastors, and countless others.

With a lifelong passion for the internal and external debates, I am going to present some of my own ideas mixed with influences from others.

I have also studied the evidence against the existence of God. I found this information underwhelming but with one persuasive piece of evidence that has, as its main strength, an undeniable emotional weight to it: the problem of evil.

You already know the following emotionally charged question, as you have likely asked yourself the very same question: How can there be a good God with the existence of evil? Though this book series is not necessarily an apologetics series, I do believe the information we will cover in the next two sections is another part of the important foundation to build upon, to then reach for what is most important in life.

This information that fueled and came from my internal and external debates lubricated the joints and movement in my life, which I'd like to share with you. This is not an academic presentation as much as a presentation of what changed me and how I have come to view things.

I will add that the material in the coming chapter, and the chapter following it, can't help but overlap and interlink. For me there is a direct link between the existence of God and what He says about Himself and us.

The coming information galloping and flying on roads we travel can help us understand and answer The Four Questions of the Apocalypse as we learn more about who sent those riders to mess with our mediocrity.

Prayer

Pause and converse with the Lord.

> *Lord,*
>
> *There has to be more than what I have been living. I want to see the evidence of You. Humble my heart to learn Your truth. I am tired of living my small life and resisting the still, small voice that tells me there is more. I want to know and live more. Show me more of You. I want more.*
>
> *Amen.*

Questions

- Why is it easier to live a convenient lie than an inconvenient truth?
- What are some convenient lies you have believed about God?
- What are some inconvenient truths you have chosen to not believe about God?
- Why do you believe in the existence of God?
- Or why do you believe that God does not exist?

CHAPTER 5
God Exists

Here are some thoughts I have chewed on, based on lifelong ideas, research, and experience. I like to put on different virtual eyeglasses to see if God exists and what He has to say. But I should be clear that because there are different pairs of glasses to view things, that does not necessarily mean that all glasses are equal in visual acuity.

If I am enjoying a beautiful hike in the Grand Canyon and I know there is someone else on my path far ahead, I can try fifty different pairs of glasses of varying prescriptions, but that does not change the fact that there is still someone ahead of me on my path, whether I can see him or not. His existence is not influenced by whether I see him or not. But if one pair of glasses is perfect for me to see him above all the other lenses, then I can see him better.

I want to show you the components of the glasses that have given me the best vision I can have at this time.

I do not know if it is normal to engage in the sheer volume of debates I have had in my head almost nonstop in my waking hours. And even in my sleep. But that is me. Perhaps I have a problem. But these internal and external discussions are a significant part of my Story. Every great story has great plot points. I will now present to you some main plot points that kept my life narrative going forward. Some of my plot points can likely be yours as well.

A Beginning to the Universe and Time

All ancient religions that I know of do not believe there was a beginning point to all of creation and time. Some ancient religions and beliefs teach that time and creation go back infinitely, so there was never a need for a beginning.

But there is one glaring exception documented thousands of years ago. In the first verse of the Bible, it states explicitly that in the beginning of time as we know it, God created the components of all of creation. Judaism and Christianity are the only ancient religions I am aware of that *originally* taught there was a God who preexisted before all of creation, who then created time and all things at a beginning point. There was a period where time and creation did not exist and in a moment the preexisting Creator created time and the essentials of creation.

There is no shortage of findings in science that presents persuasive evidence of a beginning. At its central core, the big bang theory, the most commonly held scientific belief with the most scientific evidence to back it up for the creation of the universe, along with other findings, states that there was a beginning to creation and time.[2] That instantly conflicts with other ancient religions. Several of Hugh Ross's books, as well as Fred Heeren's book *Show Me God*, among many others, clarify the theological and scientific ramifications of the idea of a beginning.

Other religions have borrowed the concept of a beginning to time and creation and took from the Jewish and Christian Scripture and attempted to make it their own.

The idea from Jewish and Christian Scripture is that God existed before creation and time and then God created creation and time in the beginning. Science discovered the evidence for

---

[2] Fred Heeren, *Show Me God* (Searchlight Publications, 1995), 131, 150, 166, 328.

a beginning thousands of years later, which included evidence like the red shifts on the light spectrum of the galaxies and stars that indicates expansion of the universe, and microwave background radiation pointing toward a great universal explosion.[3] Movement of expansion and a great explosion both indicate there had to be a beginning point.

Bottom line: If there was a beginning, there had to be a Beginner.

Creation from Nothing

At its central core, the big bang theory also states that creation initially came from nothing. Imagine that—something came from nothing! It wasn't just a magic trick but the components of the entire universe came to be from nothing in a single moment!

Of course, that sets up many problems for secular atheistic scientists, as how does a scientist, who pledges allegiance to non-spiritual material things, explain how something came from nothing?

They can't.

So that is where a spiritual realm beyond the material realm enters the picture. With the exception of Bible-based Judaism and Christianity, and any other religions that borrowed from the Bible, no other ancient religions or documents taught that God created the universe from nothing.[4]

Bottom line: How does one explain how in one moment nothing existed and then in the next moment something came from nothing?

Only God creates something from nothing.

---

[3] Hugh Ross, *The Creator and the Cosmos* (NavPress, 2001), 23, 31-32, 48-49, 221-223.

[4] Fred Heeren, *Show Me God* (Searchlight Publications, 1995), 104, 110, 131,165.

Every Day Repeating of Ordered and Structured "Miracles"

Some have made the case that if creation from nothing is of itself a sign of a God who created, how much even more significant are the almost infinite number of examples in the continued maintenance of the universe?

You would not believe me if I told you that with the passage of time, a pile of construction materials just appeared at once and then assembled itself into forming the gates and walls of Old Jerusalem. So how much less would you believe that all the parts of those same structures not only assembled themselves but, over the course of thousands of years, also self-repaired and performed self-maintenance without intelligent intervention?

Think of a cut on your finger. We expect and can even predict that it will heal. If we would never think that most machines self-create and then self-maintain themselves on a moment-by-moment basis without intelligent design and foresight, how much more should we think the same way of something even more complex than a machine, like the human brain and body? Or the universe? Even in today's era, no one would reasonably claim that AI was not at least initially intelligently designed in its beginning and that intelligence continues in its maintenance and growth.

It seems to me that God would be the best answer for creating the universe and time from nothing and also maintaining it for us on a moment-by-moment basis.

Do you have a better answer for how the universe began, came into existence from nothing, and for the moment-by-moment "self" repairs and maintenance?

The Foresight in a Fetus

Richard Wurmbrand, in his book *Tortured for Christ,* tells of his persecution and torture for his faith under communist rule. He mentions discussions that the underground church would have with those who did not believe in God.[5]

This inspired me to continue that discussion several decades later.

Why does a fetus have eyes? The fetus is in the dark and does not require eyes for survival while in the womb.

Why does a fetus have a nose? The fetus does not need a nose to survive while in the womb.

Why does a fetus have arms? The fetus does not require the use of arms for survival while in the womb.

Why does a fetus have legs? Legs serve no purpose necessary for survival while in the womb.

Why does a fetus have ears? Ears are not necessary for a fetus's survival in the womb.

Evolutionists tell us that evolution occurs without divine guidance and direction. Therefore, there is no purpose or intelligent design by an intelligent Designer. The truth is that eyes, nose, arms, legs, and ears are not needed for a fetus's survival while in the womb but would be helpful after birth. I would argue, along with others, that this shows great love, care and concern, purpose, design, and foreknowledge from a Creator God. Your birth and your life in the womb were carefully planned with a future and crafted for that time *and* for the future you who lives, sees, smells, moves, and hears today.

You are not an accident of nature.

---

[5]   Richard Wurmbrand, *Tortured for Christ,* 30th anniversary edition (Living Sacrifice Book Company, 1998).

He had plans for you even before you were in the womb.

Evolution is by definition without intelligent design and purpose. Yet a developing fetus is a perfect example of design and purpose which means there is a Designer with a purpose.

A Creator.

A God.

The Words We Use

Scientists who claim to be atheists cannot even communicate among themselves, or in their books and research, without using words that presuppose the act of creation with intelligence and intent—such as "made," "design/designed," "purpose/purposed," "create/created," "order/ordered," "numbered," "rules," "distribute/distributed," "regulate/regulated," and all the other words that cannot escape the suppressed reality for the need of a Creator and the ensuing consequences. These words, and most others used in science, presuppose a created order that then requires a Creator.

Take a careful look at the words scientists and nonscientists who do not believe in God use in everyday conversation.

We can't get away from acknowledging God. Even when we deny His existence.

The Material and Immaterial
Realms and Information

We live in the material and immaterial realms. In our everyday life, the material realm is basically that which is composed of matter—things that take up space and things we detect with our main senses: touch, sight, hearing, smell, and taste.

In most of our everyday life, the immaterial realm is composed of things that do not take up physical space and are not made of matter, such as love, the soul, the spirit, the moral law, God, Satan, and spiritual entities like angels and demons.

How do scientists who proclaim that scientific truth can only be found in the material realm explain the existence of immaterial things we know exist, such as God, love, and the soul?

Information can be immaterial. You know 1+1=2. That information you learned a long time ago is within your brain. It is a thought. It is an idea. Even after you die, the thought of 1+1=2 still exists and is still true. It is information that can be understood in your brain but exists independently apart from your brain.

What about the immaterial information within each of our cells?

Many acknowledge that there is a mix of the material and nonmaterial in the human body. Phillip E. Johnson, in his book *Defeating Darwinism by Opening Minds*, mentions evolutionary biologist George C. Williams referring to information as being nonmaterial.[6] There are the physical structures of cells within our bodies. The reality of physical and material cells within our bodies housing DNA, combined with the nonphysical and immaterial genetic information within DNA, is a great example of the material and immaterial working together. Some have used the illustration of the parts of your cell phone. There is the hardware, the physical parts, and the immaterial information stored in your phone, which is the software.

Think about the US Constitution. It is a physical document, but the heart of the Constitution are ideas, thoughts, and principles—the immaterial recorded on a material document. Think of the word "liberty" stated in the Constitution. The literal word was made of ink upon a medium to express

---

6   George C. Williams, as quoted in Phillip E. Johnson, *Defeating Darwinism by Opening Minds* (InterVarsity Press, 1997), 70.

that word. If the original document of the Constitution was destroyed in a fire, liberty would not be destroyed. Liberty is immaterial. It is separate from paper. It can be expressed in a material way, but it is immaterial.

Your DNA is full of information. It records and holds some of your data, but the data itself is a documentation of immaterial information. DNA molecules are separate from and full of immaterial information.

Some scientists would try to convince us that the only truth we can truly know—conveniently, so I would add—exists solely through science acknowledging and explaining the material realm only. What can materialistic scientists say about the truths of the immaterial, like love, liberty, compassion, the soul, and the spirit? Author, theologian, and social commentator Greg Koukl reminds us of the limitations of science with how the immaterial things in life are actually more important than the material things in life. Science doesn't tell us about the most important things.[7]

When materialistic scientists attempt to "scientifically" prove immaterial truths, have they not abandoned their highly esteemed script and role in science and attempted to take on the roles of philosophy and religion/spirituality? The attempt to change roles is in of itself an acknowledgment of the limitations of science and the existence of other vitally important roles separate from science. This change in roles and script is an admission of the existence of the immaterial, or spiritual realm.

God, who is spirit, and who created the immaterial and material, is the best explanation for the origin, maintenance, and

---

[7] Greg Koukl, "Unbelievable Unbelief," Stand to Reason, February 21, 2013, https://www.str.org/w/unbelievable-unbelief.

existence of the material and the immaterial realms. Science, through our best human efforts, falls way short of explaining God away.

Name a human being who preexisted before all things and is a better explanation for the creation and origin and maintainer of the material and immaterial realms.

The Existence of Evil Pointing to the Existence of God

Some might think that I got confused and accidentally typed in the wrong reason for the belief in God, as many believe that the existence of evil is the strongest piece of evidence *against* the existence of God.

But as many have stated before me, the ramifications and consequences of the existence of evil is actually strong evidence *for* the existence of God. Walk with me on this one.

Hard truth: You are a flawed person. Double-hard truth: The person writing this book that you hope to glean information from is also a flawed person. Is this my strange way of convincing you to have even more confidence and trust in me? What am I doing? There goes the marketing team! Uhhh . . . that would be me.

Over the years we have downloaded much information from our world, and with our data gathering from others and from ourselves, we soon figure out what we think is right and wrong.

But we are flawed. We are flawed with the data we have internalized, and we are flawed with how we interpret the data. We are biased in our storytelling and story understanding.

How are we flawed and biased? Have you ever done something wrong? Have you ever been deceived? Have you ever assumed you knew more about something and then found out you were woefully wrong? Have you ever conveniently believed something that you knew was not true or not believed in something that at some level you knew was true?

Influenced by our biases in our echo chambers, we struggle with moral truths. We are subjective beings, and our desires for power, control, love, security, significance, and influence affects how we think and what we do.

So how can we, as flawed individuals, make judgments about right and wrong that then influences others who also have the same flaws and weaknesses? And if you, a flawed person, have a different opinion about what is right and wrong in contrast to another flawed person, what makes you think that you, as a flawed person, are more right than the other flawed person? What makes you think your opinion is superior to theirs? How can I, as a flawed person, think I am right and you are wrong?

I wonder how silly we must look when we, as flawed individuals, think we are right and superior to also-flawed individuals who have an opposing opinion.

On this side of heaven, you and I will never be without flaws. What can possibly be the solution to imperfect and flawed humans finding and living perfect truth?

For us to accurately call something right or wrong requires us to appeal to a moral standard that is separate than our own. And that moral standard cannot be flawed or we are right back to the original problem of a flawed individual trying to be better than other flawed individuals. A superior and unflawed moral standard can't be human in origin if it is not going to be flawed.

We cannot call something objectively good or evil unless we have a perfect and objective standard to judge what is good or evil. Subjective humans influenced by selfish conveniences cannot be the source of this objective standard.

For us to make an objective moral judgment, like stating something is good or evil, we have to appeal to a preeminent moral law above mere flawed human subjective opinion, and a preeminent moral law requires a preeminent moral law giver.

This has to be a God without flaws.

So when we say that the existence of evil is a reason to not believe in God, would it not be more correct to say that for us to actually call something evil, we have to appeal to a preeminent moral law above our subjective convenient moral law? And a preeminent moral law points us to a preeminent moral law giver. This has to be God.

When we call something evil, we are pointing to the existence of God.

The Overwhelming Odds

I could ask you one hundred questions about me regarding information that only I would know, and you would not be able to give a single correct answer. And every other human being alive could probably ask you one hundred questions about themselves that you would not be able to answer correctly. And I would fail answering specific questions correctly about others as well.

Feeling smug and smart yet? What percentage of all that can be known about your country's history do you actually know? A neighboring country's history? Astrophysics? Physics?

What percentage of all things that can be known in the entire universe do you actually know?

I am feeling generous, so you should take advantage of that while you can. Let us say that you know .001 percent of all that can be known in the entire universe.

What are the odds of God existing in the 99.999 percent of what you don't know?

I will go with God and the overwhelming odds.

The Existence of Israel

Is there a more contested land in the universe than the Holy Land? The epicenter of spiritual/religious and prophecies, politics, and war is located in Israel, and the Holy Land is the axis of rotation of pretty much everything.

According to World Population Review, in 2025 the population in Israel is approaching ten million, and roughly about seven to eight million are Jewish.[8] According to the Pew Research Center, in 2020 the estimated number of Muslims in the Middle East and North Africa is about 414 million.[9]

Fortunately, not every person who is Muslim wants to eliminate Israel and all those who are Jewish. But if Israel is about the size of the state of New Jersey and is completely surrounded by leaders who are hostile to Israel with a 414-million to 7-million people ratio, and has few to no legitimately trusted allies (the relationship with the US and Europe waxes and wanes), you may wonder how this little country even came to be and how has it not been eliminated yet.

And if there was any doubt of intent, let us remember that human history is full of stories of nations and peoples attempting to eliminate the Jewish people and Israel from the map: Pharaoh and Haman of the Old Testament, Herod of the New Testament, all the pogroms and genocides throughout history, Adolf Hitler decades ago, and all the modern wars in the Middle East in our era—yet the country and its people continue to outlive her enemies.

---

[8] "Population of Israel," World Population Review, accessed August 26, 2025, https://worldpopulationreview.com/countries/israel,

[9] Conrad Jackett, "Islam Was the World's Fastest-Growing Religion from 2010 to 2020," Pew Research Center, June 10, 2025, https://www.pewresearch.org/short-reads/2025/06/10/islam-was-the-worlds-fastest-growing-religion-from-2010-to-2020/.

Let us pause for just a few minutes. I will wait for you as you do a quick homework assignment. Look up online *Persecution of Jews* in Wikipedia and *Antisemitism in Medieval Europe* in *Britannica.* Done? Were you surprised (but perhaps not really surprised) with our history? If the articles I mentioned are not available anymore, you should start asking why.

Humanity has a tragic and sad history of turning on one another. Every group of people can point to examples of being victims of persecution and perhaps even genocide. But antisemitism is persecution and genocide on a different level. Perhaps we need to revisit that later.

Since Israel's formal return back as a nation to the Holy Land in 1948, they have lost some battles over the years, but despite ridiculous odds in numbers, they have never lost a war. They have survived and thrived for thousands of years, outliving many of her enemies well before 1948 and after. As of this writing, since the October 7, 2023, genocide upon the Jewish people in Israel, that little country has had a strange amount of success in eliminating the leaders and followers of those who desire to destroy Israel and the Jewish people. Israel was attacked multiple times with hundreds of missiles and drones within the last few months of this writing, and Israel was virtually untouched.

And how about her history. Name another country that was exiled and dispersed from their homeland into Babylon around 600 BC and then about seventy years later brought back to their homeland and then exiled again in AD 70, to then return back to their homeland in 1948. Is there any other country in the history of the world that has been dispersed and exiled, on the verge of extinction, and then returned back to their homeland more united, not just once but twice?

And this country is special in the eyes of the God of the Bible.

I would argue that her survival against all odds, I would even say miraculous, is evidence of a God who loves her. He protects her. Though God loves all the different nations and peoples, this is different. I get the idea that her survival among all the crazy odds over all the years is by design and divine protection from a God dedicated to protect her and for all the world to witness and conclude that there is a God of Israel.

Summary of Some of My Plot Points in My Story

There you have it. Just some of the evidence of God that has dominated my internal and external discussions. There is no better explanation for God existing than a beginning to all things, creation from nothing, the miracles and maintenance of all of creation, the design and foresight for the creation of the fetus and all other creation, the inability to fully communicate without using words that presuppose the existence of God (whether we realize it or not), the creation and the existence of the material and immaterial realms, the existence of evil pointing to a necessary preeminent moral law that then points to the existence of a preeminent moral law giver, the overwhelming odds of God existing in the vast space of the lack of our knowledge, and the creation and protection of Israel.

I believe that God exists. Is the almighty, powerful God and creator of the universe unable to speak or communicate with His creation?

I am going to conclude that if there is an all-powerful God, then He would have both the ability and desire to speak and communicate with us.

A very good father would desire to have relationship and communication with his children.

Prayer

Converse with God about this chapter.

Lord,

I know You exist. But with the worries of this life, I sometimes have my times of doubt. Help me to see You even when I have times of doubt. Give me a strong faith to believe what is Your truth, and give me the boldness and courage to live out Your truth.

Amen.

Questions

- If there was a beginning to creation, does that mean there has to be a Beginner?
- Without a God, how would you explain how the universe came from nothing in a fraction of a moment?
- Without a God, how would you explain the foresight in design and purpose in a fetus?
- How would you explain the miracle of Israel?
- Do you have any spiritual sense that there must be a God? How?

CHAPTER 6
God Speaks

I believe the same God who spoke the universe and time itself from nothing into creation is able to speak. It makes sense that the God who exists, and went through all the trouble of creating all creation, has something to say.

Let's talk about you. This is a good time to consider the many times you were disappointed or downright angry when someone said something about you that simply was not true. Someone just assumed something untrue about you and never consulted with you about the real truth. Do you think it is right for people to decide who you are? Is it right for people to define you without your input? Would you be silent in each instance and allow people to decide who you are?

The simple truth is that God desires to communicate and is fully capable of communicating. That, in my opinion, is self-evident. So now we can ask, how would He communicate? Where is His message, and what would He say about Himself?

It makes sense that He would communicate through what theologians describe as "general revelation" and "special revelation." General revelation is God communicating through His creation. He can use someone in your life, the moral law, a movie, a song, the beauty and complexity of life at the cellular level, the person you love, a sunrise, or the flight of an eagle to speak to you in a deep way.

What is special revelation? Special revelation is God's direct communication providing specific information about who He is, His ways, and His creation.

There is a subjective element in sensing God communicating with us through general revelation, through His creation. To bring wholeness to communication, there must be an objective way we can know God has spoken to us. Special revelation is God communicating with us in an objective way, through His words.

My Plot Points Toward Believing the Bible Is God's Story World

I can't help but wonder that the same God who gave us a head *and* a heart would communicate with us using an objective means while utilizing our subjective senses. It makes sense that He would communicate in an objective way, free from us defining who He is. An objective spoken and written account of some sort.

I have studied many different religious documents allegedly spoken to us by God, and without hesitation I would say that the Bible has all the evidence of His Story more than any other alleged scriptures from God. Please do your own research, but from my research, when all was said and done, it was pretty easy to see the Bible as the strongest candidate for His communication to us.

I will share with you what moved the needle for me from doubt to belief and how I came to believe the Bible is God's primary communication to us, through my own thoughts and ideas mixed with some of the great influencers I mentioned before.

Once again, there is some overlap between the evidences of God's existence and the evidences of His primary communication with us. Just as it would be a great error to determine your existence, or nonexistence, by ignoring your communications, so it is with God and His communication. That is why I am unable to completely separate the evidences, as they overlap, as they do with us—the strong evidence of your existence includes your communications.

There Is Something Uniquely Different with This Story

Josh McDowell, and many others, have documented some of the numbers about the Bible that we should know. Over the course of fifteen hundred years, the Bible was written and put together with sixty-six different books, written by forty different authors, in three different languages, involving three different continents. Can you name another book written over the course of hundreds of years, composed of dozens of different authors and books, written in three different languages from three different continents, that has one unified story and message?

Let me help the skeptic answer that question: no.

It documents a Creator and a beginning to the creation of the universe and time from nothing to the distant future and how you fit in it.

I know of no ancient scriptures, other than the Bible, that claim to be from God and that originally stated, and did not borrow, that there was an already-present God who created the universe and time itself from nothing. Most ancient beliefs teach that the universe has always existed, so there was no need for a creation from nothing. Only the ancient Hebrews got the Story straight.[10] This separates the Bible from all other ancient religious texts and predates any document scientists would call science based.

Think about it. What ancient nonfiction book is there in which the author expects reverence and respect and desires to share infallibly accurate information and claims that all the components of creation came from nothing in an instant? Who would claim the essence of all creation came from nothing?

---

[10] Fred Heeren, *Show Me God* (Searchlight Publications, 1995), 104, 165.

The big bang theory, thousands of years later, came to that same conclusion.

The Bible is different.

Personal Communication like No Other

Is there another ancient book where so many people in the past and present report that while reading the Bible, the Author actively communicates, personally, in real time, life-changing truths? These truths are revealed through an entirely new sense, a spiritual sense, that is beyond and separate from our typical senses of touch, smell, taste, hearing, and sight. Truths that include transformational love and revelatory insights that re-create and change those who are immobilized or paralyzed in addiction, those who are ill, or stuck, or locked in unhealthy habits. There are new lives and new individuals with relationships healed, free from addictions, and new eyes to see victory, with new insights into how to navigate life through new freedom of movement.

There have been times when I have been reading the Bible and asked God to heal me and my healing did not come right away. Years later, I am still praying for certain issues. I do not know His timing.

And I have also personally experienced, or seen others experience, a sudden move of God. I have a friend who struggled with addiction to illegal drugs for most of his adult life, and a group of men prayed biblical truths over him—and all desire for drugs disappeared. Immediately. The ache was gone. The decades of unhealthy desire and appetite was gone in minutes, never to return.

The Author of the Bible speaks and converses through multiple dimensions, internally and externally with each individual, through His Book in real time and in any location and circumstance, like no other book or author can. You can call on the name of the biblical Author, and He is with you and conversing with you. I may like C. S. Lewis and his books from decades ago, with his wonderful truths that influence me today, but he is dead and does not personally converse with me anywhere and anytime in real time. But the God he loved and believed in does.

What other book and author communicates deep truths as if the Author Himself is right there with you, even within you?

One can read about the love of God through His words, and those same words pulsate with His life and His love, which can transform you both inside and out in a way that no mere human words could. These same words point to a God who comes down to your level to lift you up in His truth.

Documentation and Demonstration of the Immaterial and Material Realms

I believe the presence of both the material and immaterial, the natural and supernatural realms, are evidences of not only that there is a God (per the last chapter) but also that the Bible is unique in how it accurately explains better than any other communication how we live and should navigate in *both* realms.

We are both material and immaterial beings, physical and spiritual beings, moving in a world that is material, immaterial, physical, and spiritual. Is there another ancient book that has never been proven wrong that better explains life as we know it with the perfect union of both the material and immaterial realms, with objective and subjective evidence as strong as that from the Bible?

Read the book of Romans in the Bible and you will see Paul reveal the tension between the physical (the flesh) and the spirit. There is tension between wanting to do good and what we actually do. It explains the internal battle that wages within each of us. And yet on this side of heaven, God desires to use *both* the material and immaterial with the Spirit reigning within us!

How many have testified that God revealed who He was, gave supernatural counsel and guidance, while reading Scripture? Countless! I personally testify that well over 90 percent of the ideas and content of this book you are now reading is a direct result of God communicating what He wanted to communicate. This very book you are reading is evidence of the supernatural beyond my limited physical and mental abilities.

There is no better book than the Bible that explains the reality of the immaterial and material realms, which points to a communication from God.

Explanatory Power of All Things

Is there another book that has greater explanatory power than the Bible about God, Satan, how creation and time began, how something can come from nothing, love, what is good and what is not good, what went wrong, how it went wrong, how it will be fixed, the meaning and purpose of your life, and any other issue or principle you can think of?

The Bible explains better than any other document how things used to be, how things are, and how things will be better than you can dream. Looking through biblical lenses, everything we can know comes into focus better than any other religious scriptures.

Prophecy

The Bible tells you the future.

It tells you what will happen.

Think about that. Let me state it again. That Book tells you the future. It has never been wrong.

If you were to make up your own religion and your own bible, would you ever include predictive prophecies to secure your claim to truth? No. Why? Because people would be able to test those prophecies, your words, and would soon find out you were wrong. If I claimed to be God and made up my own scriptures with predictive prophecies, I would be found to be a bad god and a liar. Just interview those who know me.

That is why all other ancient religious scriptures do not make original predictive prophecies. Those religions would then be proven wrong. There is too much human power and control at stake to ever allow true testing to occur, so false religions will not play that game at all.

Some have studied and concluded that approximately 30 percent of the Bible is prophecy.[11] Considering the sheer volume of material in the Bible, that is a lot of prophecies. (If you are really interested in Bible prophecies but need someone to bring it to a layperson's understanding, in easy-to-follow-and-understand charts and diagrams, then I have found *The Non-Prophet's Guide to the End Times* by Todd Hampson to be helpful. I am hoping to touch upon biblical prophecies in this book series.)

Is there any other book where ancient writers, over the course of hundreds of years, made dozens of prophecies of a coming Savior that were then fulfilled hundreds of years later?

---

[11] Jack Kelly, "How Much of the Bible Is Prophecy," Grace thru faith, February 24, 2015, https://gracethrufaith.com/ask-a-bible-teacher/much-bible-prophecy/.

Can you think of another book where the author accurately predicted the comings and goings of world kingdoms, rulers, which countries will be blessed and cursed and why, the dots to connect to past and coming wars, a coming world ruler, the coming one-world government, one-world economy, and one-world religion, all of which is assembling right before your eyes?

What other book can inspire you to have great hope and peace in your future when the Author already has an unblemished proven track record of previous prophecies having already come true? The Author is in control of His Story. There is my hope.

If someone years ago told you one hundred precise and unique events that would occur in your life and ninety have already come true, could you believe the other ten would one day come to pass? I believe that because of the ninety, you can believe the ten.

The Bible tells us His plan and some of our future. Studying Bible prophecies leads us to believe the Bible operates outside of our familiar realm of existence. It operates outside of our known physics and time.

The Bible and its truths are beyond the limitations of the natural and material world. Therefore the Author is spiritual. He must have the ability to be outside of our realm and time domain and is supernatural like no other. It makes sense that His communication will have evidences and signs within it to prove it is a communication from God.

The Documentation of the Existence and History of Israel

What other nonfiction book prophesies the coming of a nation years in advance, a people who will be dispersed throughout the world two different times to be one day reunited back to its home, and fighting numerous wars against all odds, while surrounded and outnumbered by all nations?

I realize that I used this exact same reason in the evidence-for-God section earlier, and it also overlaps with the prophecy section. Some of the threads of the tapestry start in one section and enter other sections, as we would expect from God.

I think it belongs in both the section for the evidence for the existence of God as well as evidence that the Bible is His Story to us, because the Bible documents Israel's history and future like no other communication. I am not aware of another ancient book that documents more accurately a country's history from the start—with God and Abraham and then the lineage, history, future, and explanations for Israel's continued survival and fulfilled prophecies—than the Bible.

The Bible tells us the answers to the how, where, what, and why questions that perfectly explain the past, present, and future of the Holy Land region like no other communication. This communication is not by human origin.

Movement and Strength Navigator

I evaluate how people walk for a living. I can usually tell where in the body a person's walk is off kilter. I do this at work . . . and unfortunately, I can't help but do it everywhere I go outside of work. I have even stopped total strangers and, out of concern for how they were walking, told them where they could get help!

The Bible tells us about how and where we are walking and where we are believing our source of strength is regarding what is most important in life. Are we moving freely with our source of strength from God, or are we limited and stuck with our movement as we drain our sense of strength from ourselves? People flourish and people flounder, nations flourish and nations flounder, depending on how they are moving with or against God. The *Invisible Scar Tissue* series is a possible template, a framework, new eyes to see and navigate life that leads us walking in strength with the Author and His Story.

I know of no other book but the Bible, and its teachings and principles, that has influenced more individual people over the course of thousands of years with its movement and strength analysis (more on this in the next chapter), pointing to the ultimate source of our movement and strength. It shows us where we are experiencing spiritual atrophy and why and how to fix it.

The Bible is supernatural in its origin and is beyond any self-help book—because it is not a self-help book but a beyond-the-self book. This is contrary to everything about our society and culture because it is from God and not from mere humans.

It Documents the Most Unique Historical Figure in History, and He Affirms Scripture

Jesus is the most unique, loved, heroic, and polarizing individual to have ever lived. You would do well to claim Him as your hero above all others. Is there another book of antiquity that more accurately documents with historical and eyewitness accounts the life of Jesus, and His signs of divinity, better than the Bible? Is there another book from antiquity that better documents the hero who was to be born of a virgin, die by crucifixion, rise from the dead, and then will one day return to rule the world, all backed up with historical evidence and prophecies?

And Jesus, the most authoritative and perfect in love, power, mercy, and grace, always affirmed the previous teachings of the Bible and claimed to be the fulfillment of those very same Scriptures. Just a few of the many references include Matthew 4:4, 5:17–18, 26:55–56; Luke 24:27; John 10:35–38, 17:17.

Willingness to Die for the Bible and Its Teachings

All these reasons for the existence of God and the Bible being His communication to us has greatly influenced my beliefs in God and the Bible. But this last reason is for me perhaps the most emotionally persuasive of all.

Would you ever be willing to die for someone who claimed to be God? Would you die for the contents and message of a *Story*? Millions of Christians and Jews have refused to denounce their Author and His Story for thousands of years, which many times led to their death. It still happens today. It will still happen tomorrow. Can you name another book, story, or person that millions over the entire history of humanity have willingly chosen to die for?

There is a reason why Marxist and tyrannical regimes want to eliminate the Bible and those who believe in it and its Author. There is a reason why those who are antisemitic attack and kill the people of the Bible. I know of no other book that is more censored, criticized, ignored, and loved in history. If virtually every evil ruler in history, and in the present, have attempted to inhibit and/or destroy the Bible Story and its followers, and/or manipulate it into a different communication altogether, then I want to know *that* Author and *that* Story, for *that* Author and *that* Story proclaim liberty that mere man cannot stop. Gimmie some of that God love and God liberty! I want more of that. Many who know the love and power of God through His Word will willingly die for *that* Book and *that* Author because it is all true. And the enemies of God prove that with their responses.

There really is a God, and the Bible really is His communication.

There is a God. It makes sense to me that this all-powerful God is able to speak. That He wants to speak.

That He is speaking.

And at the same time, Someone has been presenting plot points, or perhaps dots or pixels to connect, to reveal an image of a greater Story than my own. Of all communications, it makes sense to me that the Bible, with its unique metrics, its documentation of a beginning to creation and time from nothing, is unique in that the Author speaks to the reader in multidimensional ways; explains the immaterial and material realms the best; has greater explanatory power than any other document; contains predictive prophecies that tell us the future (it tells us the future!); is a supernatural documentation of Israel, with the most unique history of any other nation; is a movement and strength navigator for life; is documentation of the most important person who has ever lived, along with His affirmation of Scripture as the Word of God—and the millions that have paid with their lives, willingly choosing to die for the contents and Author of the Bible.

There is a God.

This God speaks to us through general and special revelation.

The plot points are there. We see the dots. We see the pixels coming together. We know Someone put them there. And just like any great epic story, they must connect somehow. How do they connect? What is God saying?

What is God saying to *you*?

Prayer

Converse with the Lord on how He has communicated with you. Reading His Word and praying to Him are two keys to unlocking our freedom of movement in His strength. This book will emphasize some foundational issues to build upon as you explore the Bible and the power through prayer.

God's power flowing through your prayers will always be more powerful than any of my words.

Lord,
You are alive. You speak. Tell me what You have to say to me through Your Word, through Your creation. Show me You are real, and show me who You are. Speak, for Your servant is listening.
Amen.

Questions

- Can you name a being, other than God, who could have written a Story over the course of fifteen hundred years and who can personally communicate with you today?
- Can you name another book that can tell the future without ever being wrong?
- Can a country with Israel's history ever exist without a God?
- What can I learn from all the millions of people throughout history who were willing, and are still willing, to die for a book and its message?

CHAPTER 7

What You Love Determines Your Movement and Strength

I have summarized where we are so far with the information in this book in diagram 1.

At the top of the diagram, you will see that it always comes back to Story. There you are at the bottom, raising your hands up, perhaps surrendering and reaching for what is above and beyond you. We have answered the four questions, and perhaps our vision is clearer to see that we each mostly center our life around ourself.

Truth be told, you are probably like me. You can't get into other peoples' heads and see through their eyes. From your perspective, life ultimately revolves around you. Perhaps in response to spiritual injuries from your own sins and those committed against you, you increased your focus upon yourself out of a sense of self-preservation. And after the trauma(s), like an old physical injury, internal scar tissue laid down to limit painful movement, which then limits our normal and healthy movement and strength.

But now you are limited in movement, and you now have an altered movement pattern. How do I know this? Again, I'm just like you.

And if this is all true, is it difficult to imagine why we have challenges with our relationships? With each wounded person living this self-centered small way, there will be differences in self-centered opinions among the wounded.

It Always Comes Back to Story

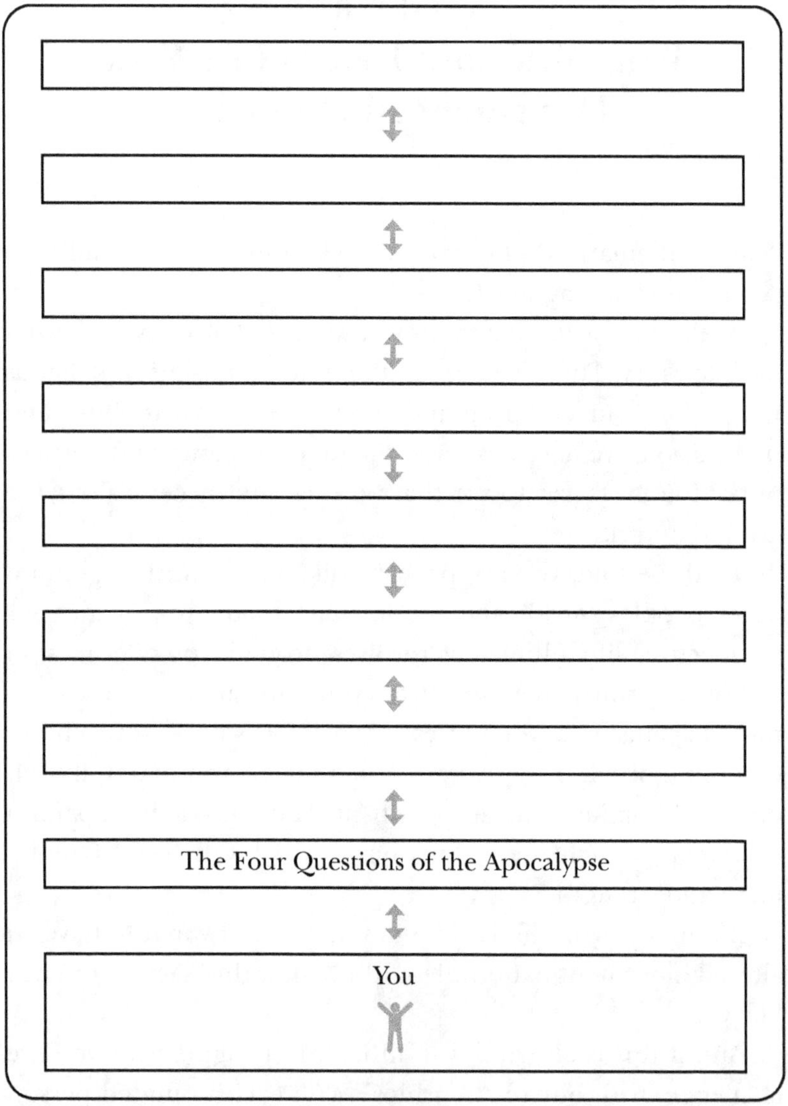

↕

↕

↕

↕

↕

↕

The Four Questions of the Apocalypse

↕

You

Diagram 1

Can there ever be love and a constant totality of peace in our relationships when each person has made themself the center of the world in most circumstances?

Hopefully, you and I can see that something is not right with our self-centered life. Something is off within ourselves. We have a lack of wisdom, love, joy, peace, patience, self-control, and fulfillment, if we are honest. We are stuck and locked into our broken ways.

But there is great news. Let us push the fear of death and the effects of sin to the side. There is something beyond us. Something beyond our tiny story with tiny views.

As we covered in the previous two chapters, there is a God and He has spoken. He speaks. He has communicated with us in the Bible who He is and who we are, and He continues to communicate today so we can get unstuck, freed up from our rigid, stiff, selfish, and broken ways.

There must be a way for us to walk toward what is ultimately most important in life.

Movement and Strength Analysis (Gen. 3; Matt. 7:13–14; Rom. 1:18–25; 2 Cor. 4:7; Gal. 5:1, 7, 16, 25; Eph. 2:10, 3:16, 20)

Love is in the air.

But what do we love?

Patients with pain can often have rigid, stiff, or paralysis of movement. As a physical therapist, I assess movement and strength with every patient. With athletes, I must consider explosive power with running and jumping. This, combined with them telling me about themselves, helps me to help them. If they have pain, I will likely find deficits in normal movement and strength.

They often all come together in a costly combo plate that each person would love to return for their money back.

With chronic pain patients, I will often find habits such as poor posture, malalignment of different bones, poor body mechanics, and suboptimal movement and strength patterns. Pain can force adaptive and modified lifestyles responses. Whether they realize it or not, they now move differently. Perhaps they move less often. They have lost normal movement. Or perhaps there is now a strategy of not moving that part of the body at all.

With time, loss of range of motion and strength in one body part means other body parts may end up with increased use and overuse, resulting in pain in new areas. All these factors can lead to changes in how people walk, and then a cycle can kick into a new gear, as poor walking mechanics can over time lead to pain and loss of normal movement in other body parts, and the new pains can then further alter walking mechanics.

So what does pain and loss of movement, strength, and power have to do with love and God? We can lose or gain movement and strength in our relationship with God. In God's Story for us, shortly after Adam and Eve ate from the tree of knowledge of good and evil (they attempted to live the tiny vision of their desires being above God's), they heard God walking in the garden. Imagine hearing the sound of God walking in His garden!

Now imagine not being able to walk with your longtime friend or, in some cases, your furry friend, like you used to. I was blessed to walk with my rescue dog, Rosie, for fourteen years. Fourteen years! She was such a faithful friend. I miss her.

Now imagine not being able to walk side by side with God as you once did since you were created.

Adam and Eve, now with a newfound shame that did not exist before they disobeyed God, hid themselves among the trees. Then God called out to Adam. I imagine this to be the most heartbreaking of questions that God has ever asked, though He already knew the devastating answer: "Where are you?" (Gen. 3:9)

After reading God's first question, I then fast-forward to Paul speaking about God to those seeking spiritual truths: For in him we live and move and exist (Acts 17:28).

Movement is important. Movement is implied with that first question from God. Why would He ask "Where are you?" if there had not been any movement? God asking this question implies there is movement toward and movement away from God. Paul said years later we move and live and exist in God. As a PT I can relate to movement and living.

After Adam and Eve believed the serpent and disobeyed God, He knew where they were. They had moved away from Him. They had literally walked away from Him to hide in fear for the first time in human history. Note the connection between walking away from God for the first time and fear entering our world for the first time.

How did toxic fear come to be, and where did it come from? Toxic fear did not exist before we walked away from God. I define toxic fear as a fear not from God. It is a fear from the enemy of your soul wanting to torment and destroy you.

Do you struggle with toxic fear?

Adam and Eve chose to exercise their freedom and moved away from their Creator Father and attempted to gather strength and movement apart from God. They chose another. They chose creation, which included themselves and Satan, above God the Creator. God asked His question like a faithful lover asking why His love had chosen someone else above Him.

Now look at diagram 2. I now propose a possible model of our movement and strength as we walk toward or away from God.

It is an issue of love.

What do we love?

It Always Comes Back to Story

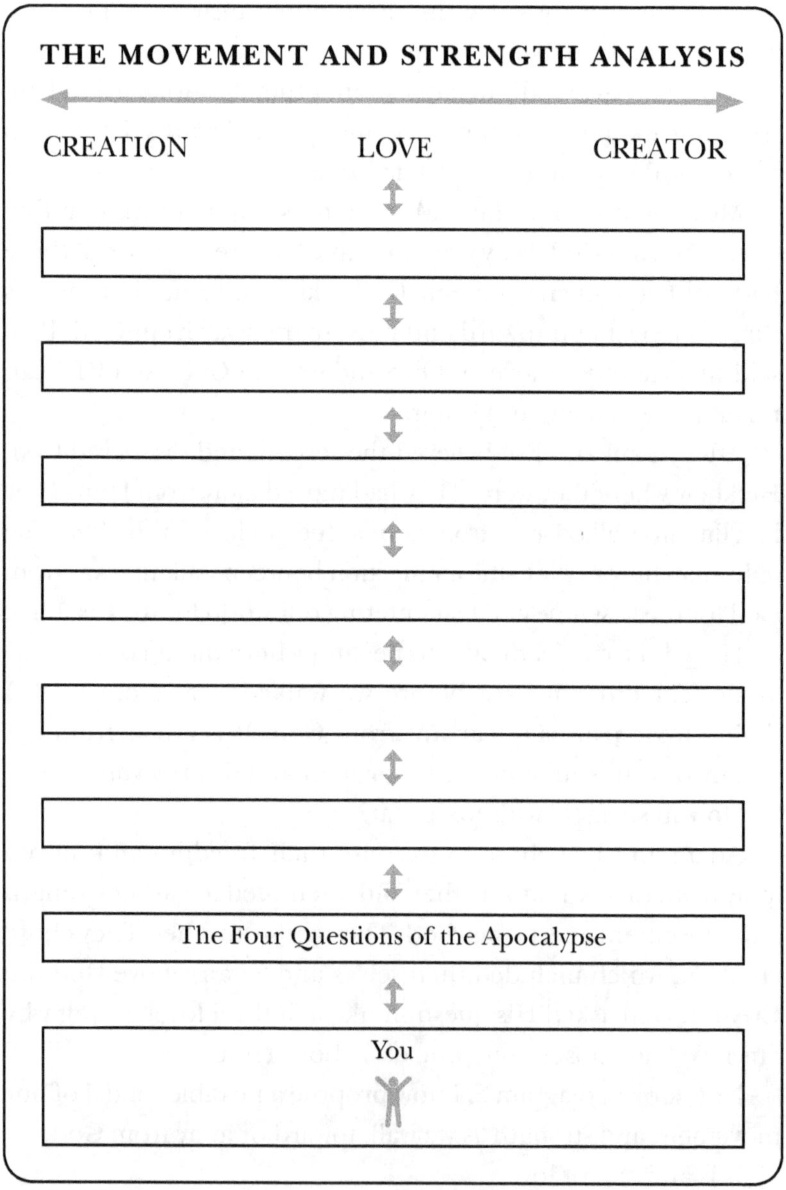

THE MOVEMENT AND STRENGTH ANALYSIS

CREATION   LOVE   CREATOR

The Four Questions of the Apocalypse

You

Diagram 2

Near the top of the diagram, the continuum scale moves from one side to the other, as we rarely stay static. We place our love somewhere at all times. Are you moving toward creation as your god or the Creator as your God?

Where do you place your ultimate love? Where do you seek your primary source of liberty of movement, strength, and power? Do you seek liberty of movement and your strength primarily from creation (yourself, other people, work, your material things, money, drugs, alcohol, sex, food) or the Creator? Please don't misunderstand my intentions. God's creation was originally created to be good. And we should freely partake in His wondrous creation, but it should not be our god above God.

As you consider where you are on the movement and assessment scale, are you stuck in invisible scar tissue from prior injuries and wounds, from sins committed by and against you affecting your spirit? All of this can then affect who you think you are.

Creation Is God

Let's look at the opposite ends on the Movement and Strength Analysis scale of what we love, near the top of the updated diagram. If we gravitate to the left on the diagram, we move toward making creation our god.

Have you noticed how it seems that everything is aligned against you when you try to eat healthy? You may feel that the entire system is rigged against you.

Compared to eating junk food, eating healthier is more work, more expensive, less available, less convenient, in most instances does not taste as good, and it isolates you when eating with others. There is a great resistance to eating healthy.

Have you ever attempted to exercise more regularly? Compared to sleeping in or being unnecessarily leashed to an electronic device, trying to exercise regularly takes more time; is more physically, mentally, and emotionally demanding; and can cause some degree of physical discomfort. There is a great resistance to exercising regularly.

Have you ever tried to be more financially disciplined and actually followed a good budget?

Have you ever known that you should apologize and ask forgiveness to that friend or loved one whom you wronged, but how much easier it is to come up with reasons to justify your actions or words?

You get the idea. The list goes on and on.

You and I often resist doing what we know is right and good. It is usually easier to do the opposite.

It is always easier to move toward the left on the scale and make creation our god, and it is always more difficult to move to the right on the scale.

Why? There is a haunting secret that you already know. You know that familiar daily resistance to what is good for you. It happens because you are not alone. You are not alone behind enemy lines.

Your enemy is with you.

Your enemy is within you.

If you thought the system was rigged against you trying to eat healthy, exercise, and be more financially disciplined, trying to live with the Creator as your God is exponentially more difficult.

Think about it. How have you been trained since your youth? Did your culture, family, and friends teach you to seek creation (e.g., the worship of yourself, money, drugs, sex, work, a celebrity, a musician, a politician, a political party, a teacher, occult practices) above God in most matters? Did your schools and teachers and professors teach you to seek Creator over creation? In public education, how long would your teacher have had a job if they actively taught you to love and obey God above all others and all things?

Do your favorite movies, TV programs, news programs, musicians, celebrities, teach you to seek the Creator over creation? Most secular creative content creators would not have a job if they did. They would lose money, influence, and popularity if they suddenly switched to proclaiming Creator over creation.

What would happen to the career of the most popular pop artist you can think of if she suddenly used her art to influence others to follow God above all things? Including placing God above herself and her own art—which would then affect her financial accounts and her influence and those who make money through her? She would soon find out who really loved her. Though God is ultimately in control, her career would be over as she once knew it. That is tremendous pressure to conform.

There have always been small pockets of resistance to drifting to the left on this scale, but these, again, are small pockets. It is so much easier to just pick creation over Creator whenever it is convenient to gain or maintain power, control, finances, career, influence, and pleasure. We usually do what we were trained to do and act out what feels right and go along with what everyone else is doing. Try and make a bold proclamation of God in all arenas of your life and see what happens.

At the core, you and I live out moment by moment what Adam and Eve lived out in the garden with Satan. We sin because we choose to believe "I am God" versus submitting our lives to God, who proclaims "I am God." I make the default choices that conveniently seem to place me on the throne of my life. And sorry to tell you, but you do this too.

The Creator Is God

If you look in the opposite direction to the right, you will see the opposite end of individual heart allegiance. We already went over some of the plot points that point me to the existence of God, and I have to say it is much stronger than the evidence against the existence of God. It seems that it should be the most obvious of truths, but it is worth repeating what should be self-evident of all self-evident truths:

God is God.

Wow! It even feels just plain silly typing "God is God," but my dark secret is yours. We don't always live what is obviously true. Sometimes we don't want the light of the truth shining on us. Sometimes we walk away from God and try to hide in the dark or behind the trees and cover our nakedness with flimsy excuses.

And that is the cosmic universal battle. It is creation saying "I am God" versus the Creator saying "I am God." Which path do I choose? The one you choose will determine the trajectory of everything for you.

Which is it?

Creator.

Creation.

I must clarify that even someone who lives the life choice of Creator over creation still lives with and operates in life with creation. I still try to earn more money and use my car and pay for fuel and maintenance, but does the pursuit of money and my things rule over me as my god? I am not saying that a true Christian does not utilize creation, of course, but I am saying that our true heart allegiance cannot be equally both Creator and creation.

We live on a continuum, a journey. Sometimes we are overall trending to the left and sometimes to the right. Even within the same individual, one may walk the wrong direction on a specific issue, while their life is in sync with God in other issues. There is not only a cosmic battle throughout but a civil war battle within each individual.

Ultimately, it is about what we love the most.

So let's look at our diagram 2 again.

Above us is the truth that it always comes back to Story. That is you at the bottom, with your hands raised up, asking for help, or perhaps raised out of frustration—or both.

And the bad news is, you are not alone. You have an adversary and his proxies with you, which resist everything good in your life. They whisper into you to follow the self-love and god of self in your heart. They tell you that you are not being true to *yourself* if you don't follow *your* heart.

The whole system seems rigged for you to fail.

But you are responsible and accountable for your decisions.

Now on our diagram, we have the Movement and Strength Analysis, which can help us analyze where we are moving, where we seek our strength/power—toward creation above all things or toward the Creator, who is above all things.

We have connected some dots. We put together a few pixels of the overall picture. But there is more.

There is a major concern.

No matter how hard you try, you can't live as you were created to live.

We can't do this right.

We need help.

It Always Comes Back to Story

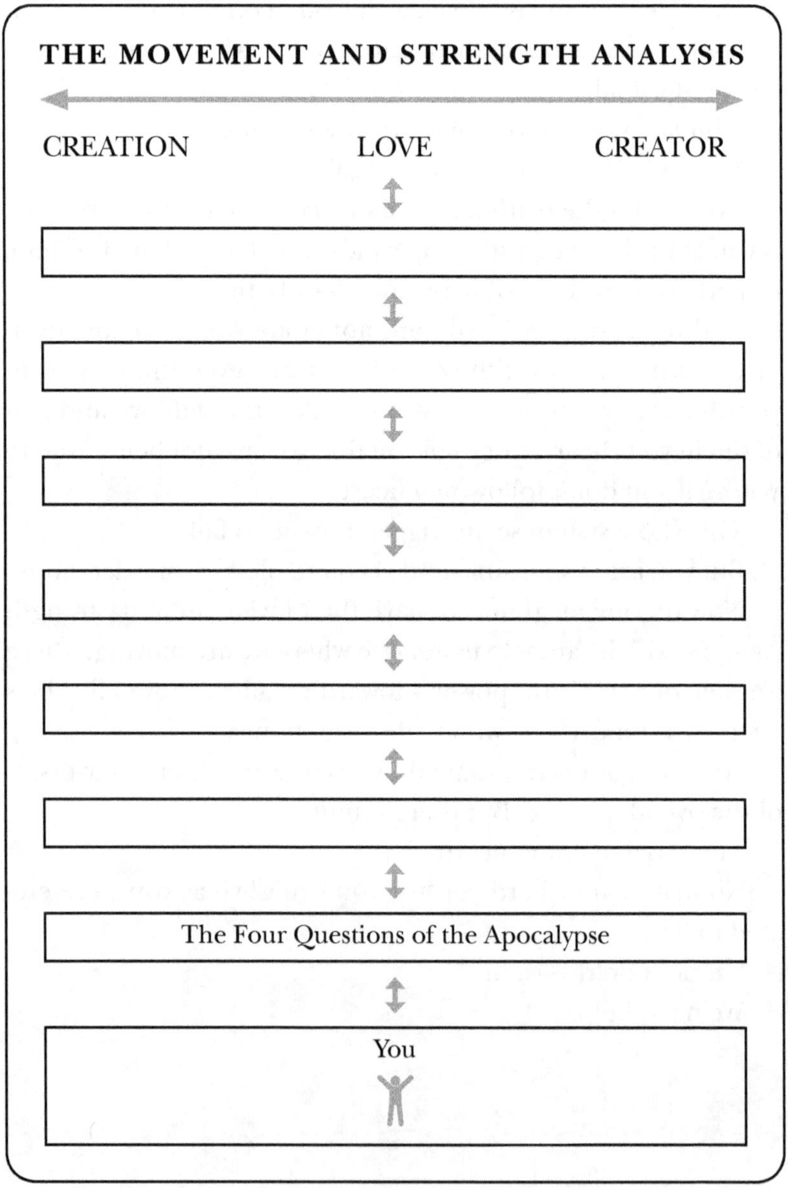

THE MOVEMENT AND STRENGTH ANALYSIS

CREATION   LOVE   CREATOR

The Four Questions of the Apocalypse

You

Diagram 2

Prayer

Converse with God about what you love most and where you ultimately seek movement and strength from.

Lord,

I confess to You that I have lived the big lie and the small life of me above You. I have placed my love, my heart's allegiance, in the wrong place. Forgive me for living the little story when I know You have a meta Epic before me. I turn away from the small days and ask you to guide me into the coming epic days.

Exercise your will within me.

Amen.

Questions

- Where are you?
- In what ways have you lived the self-centered life?
- Are there people you need to ask forgiveness from when you unnecessarily placed yourself above someone else?
- Are there people you need to forgive when they unnecessarily placed themselves above you?
- What is one thing you would ask of your Author?

CHAPTER 8

What Is Most Important in Life

Now is a great time to revisit the fourth of the Four Questions of the Apocalypse upon Mediocrity.

When I got that surprising and yet semi-expected phone call that my father had died, I will never forget that within minutes the immediate family gathered around his bed. I will also never forget the last expression on my father's face. My father appeared to be frozen in time, either in the process of closing his eyes to go to sleep or opening his eyes as if waking up.

Was my father closing his eyes for his final rest on earth, or was he waking up for the first time to a new life?

Over the next few hours, we gathered in sadness. We wiped our tears. We laughed at some stories of good times with my dad. I even learned new stories about my dad that I did not know. Though my dad was with God, he knew beforehand the love and the precious relationships that were represented around him.

There was healing for me around my father's old and broken-down earth suit, only this time fear of death did not enter me. This time I appreciated the brevity of life and was more free with how to live in my final days.

What is most important in life?

As I continue to get older, I can honestly say it is my loved ones gathered together for a great meal or simply to be together with my friends and my acquaintances. Today, and in my final hours, it is going to be the love and relationships I have had in my life.

If I had to describe the Bible in one word, I would say "love." Wait, I would say "relationships." Wait again. I would have to change the rules from one word to say "love in relationships."

I want to clarify that I do not mean just romantic love but the love that one has for family, friends, coworkers, neighbors, pets . . .

The Bible describes who God is, who we are, and what creation overall is. It puts into order for us how everything intersects and fits, as it is meant to all tie together with love in our relationships.

Do you really need further evidence?

Homework

I have a short homework assignment from your PT that incorporates a different type of movement—the movement and growth in relationships. The "Harvard Study of Adult Development" is a longitudinal study that has been ongoing since the late 1930s and has been acquiring data for decades. Watch the TED Talk video *What Makes a Good Life? Lessons from the Longest Study on Happiness.*[12]

Let's pause for a few minutes to let you do your exercise.

Done? What did you think? The information was probably both surprising and expected. There is a relationship between love, your relationships, and your sense of happiness. Probably confirmation of what you already knew or suspected, but still great to be reminded.

---

[12]   Robert Waldinger, *What Makes a Good Life? Lessons from the Longest Study on Happiness,* TED Talk, 12 min., 46 sec., YouTube, posted January 25, 2016, https://www.youtube. com/watch?v=8KkKuTCFvzI.

What Is Most Important in Life? The Most Important Is Love and Relationships (Ex. 20:3; Luke 10:17–20)

Love and relationships. Though two elements, I used a singular verb (is) in the subhead title because they are so tightly linked. All this information, and my story about my dad, and "the deathbed test" I mentioned earlier, is all confirmation of what I suspect you already know. But oh, how we need to be continually reminded when the adversary with us distracts and convinces us otherwise.

Riding upon one of our horses of the apocalypse, pounding on mediocrity and cutting through the night holding a dying light, you may be able to see the embers of the light grow as we further reduce to the core of the core of what is most important of what is most important.

What is the most important love and relationship we can have?

True, it is vital to have the right relationship with ourselves. If you hate yourself, there will be problems. Swinging too far in the opposite direction with toxic self-love can be a problem too.

But if there is a Creator God, and there is, and God is both love and the creator of love and those we love, does it not make sense to choose the Creator over all creation as what is ultimately most important?

Think about it. If you get the order of Creator over creation out of whack and place yourself or your significant other above God, what will happen? With toxic self-love, the terms *narcissist, sociopath,* and *psychopath* come to mind. I pray for your significant other if you place them as your god. I need prayer if I place my children as my god. Imagine the horrific consequences and unnecessary pressures on you as a spouse, or as a child, when someone places you as god in a relationship. No one can live up to that. No one should have to try to live up to that.

If we place money above God, or as our god, what will eventually happen? If we place power or control or sex above God, what will eventually happen? Does the word *slavery* come to mind? Slavery is another way of saying little to no freedom of movement, and without strength to live freely, we become rigid and stuck, paralyzed with little to no liberty.

Your significant other will never be as good as God. My children will never be able to live up to the expectations of being God. You will never have enough power and control to fill within you what only God can fill. Sex will always fall short of God. And . . . I shudder to think what happens when the temporary existence of your significant other, your children, your money, your power, your control, your own health, your ability to have sex is no longer there for you. How utterly depressing to live the small life.

Only God can eternally exist well past your temporary never-to-fully-satisfy fixes. It makes sense to make God the preeminent love relationship above all others.

Take a look at our updated diagram number 3.

Now we have what is most important hovering above us as we, below, try to reach for it.

How do we get to what is most important in life?

It Always Comes Back to Story

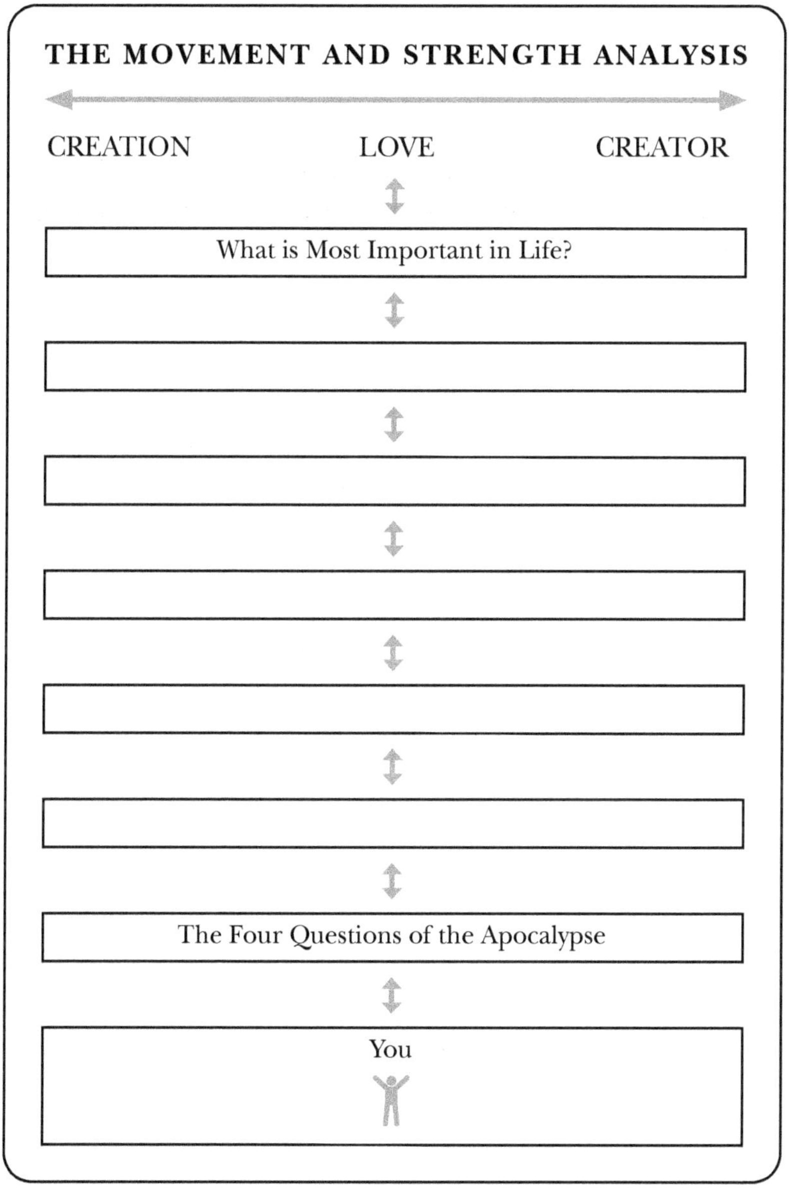

THE MOVEMENT AND STRENGTH ANALYSIS

CREATION   LOVE   CREATOR

What is Most Important in Life?

The Four Questions of the Apocalypse

You

Diagram 3

Prayer

Lord,

Help me to find what is most important in life. Help me to recalibrate, to reboot my life to then walk toward what is most important. Lead me where You want me to be. I am tired of living what I used to think was most important. I will never be God. You are God. Take my hand and walk with me.

Amen.

Questions

- What is most important in your life?
- Where is there an inconsistency in your life with actually living out what is most important?
- If you had to describe what you know of the Bible in one word, what word would you use?
- What thoughts did you have regarding the happiness study?
- How are you feeling about the trajectory in living your life?

CHAPTER 9

Level I and Level II Truth Modes

There is a God. He speaks. He has spoken and continues to speak to us through general and special revelation.

At the top of our updated diagram 3, it all comes back to Story. There is a God-made movement and strength analysis assessment in which God evaluates where our walk is heading, where we ultimately place our love, and where we seek our movement and strength. Is our love misplaced? Is creation our god or the Creator our God?

The Four Questions of the Apocalypse exposes and judges our mediocrity and status quo. The love in our relationship with God is above all other important loves and relationships with others.

There you are at the bottom of the diagram, with your arms lifted high . . . and you are not alone. We have an adversary resisting everything good for us.

We can see if we are trending to the left or toward the right of our Movement and Strength Analysis diagram.

How do we navigate from the bottom to up and toward that which is most important in life?

I have gone through some stages in my life that I would like to share with you, as you and I are similar in many ways. I want to propose four levels of awareness of truth, with some biblical support, that help us navigate and move freely and with more strength.

Level One Truth: Self Mode
(Gen. 2:7, 20–25; 3:6, 16–21)

Self mode is where we all start. As a baby you cried when you were hungry, had a full diaper, were tired, or for any other reason that your confused parent(s) couldn't figure out. You cried because you wanted something.

As a toddler, if some miniature tyrant took your toy away in preschool, you let the justice of a child's anger rule and reign, you accepted it, or you cried, or all the above.

As we get older, our self-centered ways get more stealthy and creative. Folded arms. The silent treatment in passive aggression. Gossiping. We are creative.

We should each be congratulated. We each recognize and understand there is a self that is different and separate from others. That is a good thing.

Think how strange and difficult life would be if you could not separate yourself from others around you. It might at first seem noble to think you are every other person, but imagine living your life totally dependent on what others think and do apart from your own desires, hopes, and dreams.

Imagine living life never confronting a wrong committed against you personally, or anyone else, because we are all just one biological blob. Where is the diversity in that scenario?

Awareness of the individual self is necessary for the health of the group.

But problems eventually arise when we get stuck, like a scar-tissue-fused joint, and we get caught in a pattern of not being able to move past what our leash of selfishness allows. Some of us, to varying degrees, never move past looking at life and others strictly through only our own eyes, too often with little to no regard for others. The self that is left unchecked becomes a narcissist, sociopath, or a psychopath.

The Bible is full of examples that note we are separate individuals. We see the first instance of human individuality all the way back in Genesis 2. God formed a man and determined that he should not be alone, then He formed a woman. Note they are separate individuals. Later they are joined as one. They had to be separate individuals to then be joined as one. The rest of the Story continues the theme of individuals and how each individual sees himself/herself in relation to others and God.

Level Two Truth: Student Mode (Job 38, 39, 42; Eccl 4:13; Jer. 32:33; Matt. 11:29; Luke 6:40; Gal. 3:24; 1 John 4:1)

Ask any PT and they can tell you of instances where the patient thinks they know more than the PT and how to treat their condition. Some will even try to convince the PT to treat them the way they think they should be rehabilitated. Sometimes they are right. And sometimes the patient comes in with a self-prescribed diagnosis and how to fix it, and if the PT's idea does not align with the self-prescribed diagnosis, the PT has a difficult time convincing them to pursue a course of treatment that is counter to the patient's own program. With their preconception of what is wrong, they can then decide not to fully comply with what the PT prescribes and then get frustrated with their lack of progress in a self-fulfilled prophecy.

Unfortunately, it is also true that there are times when the PT is not seeing the truth of the patient's condition and the patient picks up on this. The PT can think a certain way and not be open to the possibility that they could be wrong, and that does not instill confidence in the patient, which will affect results.

Perceptive patients then move on to another PT, or another form of treatment, or just stop trying.

I propose that what is helpful is if the patient and the health practitioner both move through a student mode.

Student mode is when a person moves forward with their experiences and what they know so far but navigate with the realization they could be mistaken, as they are still learning. There are two main parts of student mode that are both necessary to move freely and in strength.

Humility

Your PT is now asking you to do a homework assignment. Read Job 38 and 39 in the Bible.

Done? Job and his friends seem to think they have things figured out regarding Job's misfortunes. Then God responds to Job. This turns out to be an old-fashioned, loving, verbal beatdown that cannot be countered. God is God and He is being real with them. He is basically saying, "I am God and you are not. Sit at my feet and I will teach you. Close your mouth. Open your hardened heart. Learn."

In Job 42 Job demonstrates a soft and humble heart and responds to God similar to how a student acknowledges a truly great teacher full of wisdom. God's ways are far above our own and remind us that our Creator Father and God is above all, and that should humble us as a student to pay attention to the Master Teacher.

I am not sure it is possible to consistently learn without the humility of acknowledging that one has an absence of knowledge. If I enroll in a class and think I know more about the subject than the idiot teacher in front of me, I will have a difficult time learning anything.

This is not student mode.

But if I enter into the class in the full humility of knowing I do not know everything, and wanting to learn everything I can from the teacher, I will learn.

Testing

For many of us, our greatest seasons of learning and growing come during great trial and testing. To be a good student and learner, I have to be tested. Every legitimate degree in education involves thorough testing of the student's knowledge—and if a person has a certain educational degree, they have passed extensive testing of their knowledge.

What person has ever gained a high level of skill in *anything* without some form of testing? Perhaps it is with formal testing, or maybe through trial and error, which require correction to then do the activity better.

Here is a simple way to test whether you are regularly living in the student mode. Pick a hot topic. Religion, politics, finances, Marxism, antisemitism, capitalism, abortion, gender identity, sex outside marriage. Now ask yourself, "Do I honestly believe there is a possibility I could be wrong about my beliefs? When was the last time I sought out and honestly considered an articulate argument against what I believe?"

God instructs us to test the spirits to see if they are from God. If you do not seek out regular challenges and testing of your beliefs, then you are probably living with confirmation bias in your echo chamber.

That is not student mode.

We will be stuck in our ways and impaired in our movements and strength in our relationships if we don't get the student mode down. How far will you get with loved ones without love and humility and the honest testing of what you believe?

Let's look at diagram 4 now.

It Always Comes Back to Story

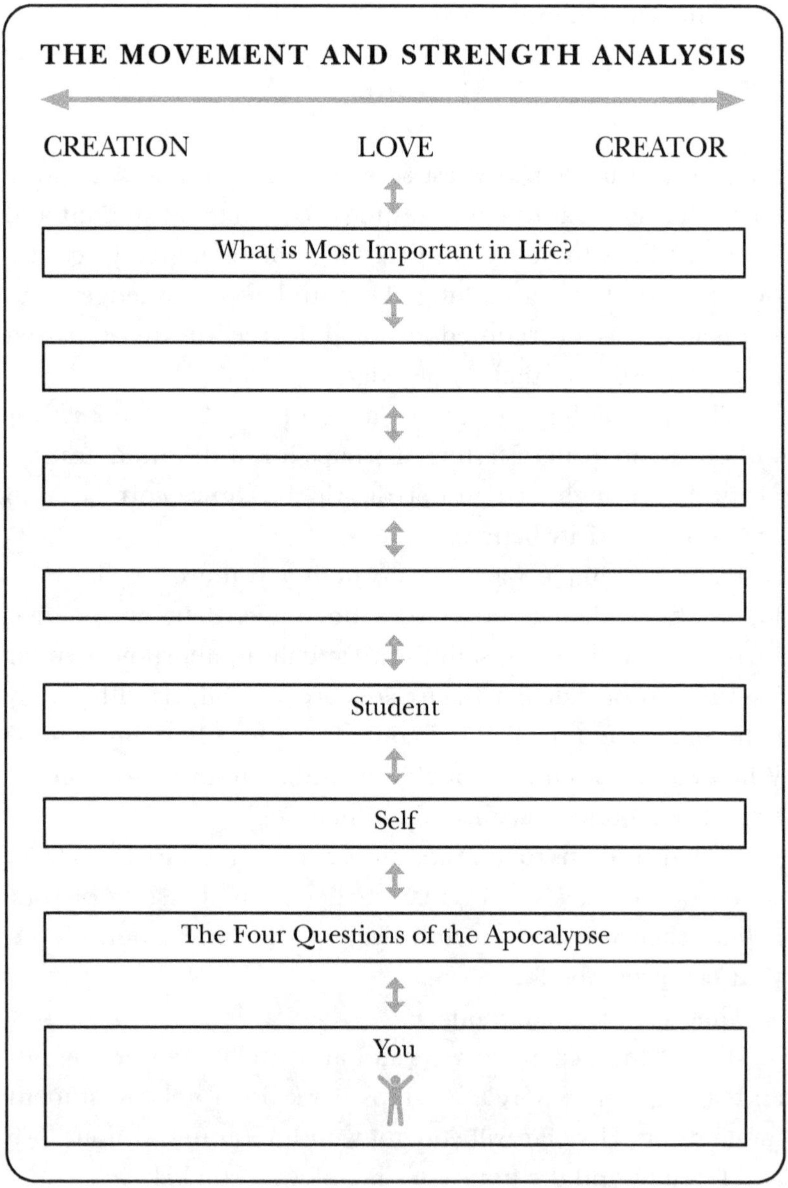

THE MOVEMENT AND STRENGTH ANALYSIS

CREATION   LOVE   CREATOR

What is Most Important in Life?

Student

Self

The Four Questions of the Apocalypse

You

Diagram 4

You are now reaching for something bigger than yourself. How do you get to what is most important?

Prayer

Lord,

Grow me past my old life of seeing and living only through my eyes and desires. Raise me up as a student of the living God. Show me how to sit at Your feet in full humility and testing all that I believe to follow You with all that I am. I am tired of majoring in me and minoring in truth, and I desire to follow my Master Teacher. I trust You to test me and my ideas so I can major in You.

Amen.

Questions

- What areas in your life is it easier to be free from being stuck in self mode?
- What areas in your life do you struggle with the default self program?
- Do you actively try to test your beliefs? How do you do this?
- When was the last time you changed your mind after finding information that challenged your way of thinking? What was the topic?
- How does your culture train you to be humble or arrogant?

CHAPTER 10

Level III Truth Mode

We have so far covered two modes of moving in truth. Moving from self to student now moves us to the next truth mode:

Level Three Truth: Story Mode (Gen. 1:1; Acts 7; Gal. 3:29; Eph. 3:14–15; Heb. 2:10, 12:2).

It always comes back to Story.

Let's spend some time with how we assemble the data in our lives and turn it into backstory, plot points, and plot twists, which provide the framework for how we move from moment to moment in our days.

Importance of Story

I told you about the fear and pain in my life and the discovery of how this affected me with the loss of healthy movement and strength. I also shared how studying and practicing as a physical therapist was a major influence in my life.

I would like to share with you a second major influence. I love stories. You do too. We think and process all information into the form of story in our heads. We make sense of *everything* through the structure of story. Did I say *everything?* Yes, I said *everything.* Surely I must have meant most things, right? No. I said *everything.* At least *everything* I can think of.

As I mentioned before, when you were an infant, you cried when you were hungry, tired, not feeling well, bored, or weighed down with an uncomfortable, heavy, soggy, smelly diaper. (How can something so offensive come out of a beautiful baby?) Under good circumstances, a loved one would have attended to you and cared for you. You learned you were an individual and could get attention from other individuals when you cried for it.

Without even realizing it, you eventually formed parts of a story in your head that connected your cry with getting attention. Hopefully, you learned love, affection, and comfort during those trying times. You learned how to implement the principle of cause and effect. Get attention and feel better.

Under most circumstances, this strategy of demanding attention and then getting what we wanted worked. That strategy was necessary in those early years. It probably worked so well that as we grew up, our parents tried to teach us to focus less on our own selfish narrative and to see life through other people's eyes to better understand their stories apart from our own.

Unfortunately, we make bad decisions, and not all of us had the healthy family dynamics or environment to live life considering others. We still have remnants of the infant / young child demanding attention above others. We never quite fully grew up. You and I each have a remaining default program of self-centeredness that varies in strength.

It is important to understand the importance of Story and getting our stories straight, as our story making can give us an accurate way to understand and navigate life.

We Love Stories

Just how important is the principle of story? We love watching movies and our favorite TV programs. Some love to read a great novel. You communicate with family and friends to hear their story updates or to give an update on your unfolding tale.

We usually enjoy meeting a fascinating person and hearing about their unique experiences. Think about it. When you hear someone talking on a podcast, in a message at church, in an online video, or giving a lesson, what is it that you remember the most?

Yup.

Stories.

Interestingly, Jesus, the most famous person who ever lived, often taught through stories. He knew what he was doing. As a matter of fact, the Old Testament and New Testament are primarily stories within a greater Story.

We use stories to make sense of the world we navigate. We, in essence, put on glasses to see and observe life in front of us and then put that data into our heads in the form of stories.

What am I talking about?

Right now as you are reading this book, both you and I are intersecting in a fascinating way. While you are reading parts of my story written for you, you are composing a story about me. You've already made decisions and judgments about what I am writing and about my personality based on the story you've composed in your head, along with how life operates and your previous experiences with other people. You may have already decided that you like me or, perhaps, not so much. Perhaps you are reserving full judgment for later. But you have still made judgments nonetheless. This is not necessarily a bad thing. That is how you make sense of what I have written when compared to your own narrative.

Think of how you even got this book. It was based on a previous experience where you purchased a book before. If this book was gifted to you, how did you even know what a gift was or what a book was, if not based on previous data entered into your expanding tale?

Let's back this up even further. How did you even learn how to read? In your backstory, people taught you the alphabet and then you learned to combine the letters into words and sentences. In the ongoing process of learning how to read and write, you performed flashbacks in your story to remember and utilize past lessons, and you brought that information to the present to then build upon for the future. Over time, lessons learned in your present were built upon past lessons to prepare you for future lessons. That in itself is a great story!

But there is more. There is another side. In my mind as an author, I have composed a narrative in my head of a possible typical reader of this book, and I've written with that hypothetical reader in mind. I am using the data I have composed in my head based on those I have interacted with into a book, attempting to intersect with you.

When you are on a date, or spending time with a loved one or friend, are you not composing a story or adding to what you are composing about the individual(s) you are with? Are they not doing the same thing regarding you?

I had been driving for decades and had never been in a car accident. That changed a few weeks ago. I was driving on a major freeway and took an exit that had two lanes. As I was in the far right lane, another driver cut across the freeway in order to not miss the exit and crossed over two lanes and hit my car on the driver's side. I never had a chance to avoid it.

I knew enough to pull onto the shoulder, as did the other driver. I sat there stunned for a few seconds, wondering what I should do next. Why did I have that pause? I had never been in an accident before, so I did not have that experience in my story. It was a new encounter. Writing a quick new entry into my story takes time. I imagine that if I had been in previous accidents, I would have had more data to react upon more quickly.

It has been said that thoughts create actions and actions create behaviors and behaviors create character. You edit the stories in your head all the time. You can choose to move past certain thoughts, or you can choose to not edit and actually feed the unedited thoughts, for better or worse.

Going back to our Movement and Strength Assessment scale, you can choose your love and choose to see life primarily through the eyes of the Creator or through the eyes of creation. The narrative you are composing is influenced by the pair of lenses you choose to see with. Your beliefs about God, Satan, who you are, what is good and bad, right and wrong, your politics, your personal philosophy and beliefs are all processed through the edited or unedited story you compose every moment of every day.

But what if you are wrong about your stories? Have you ever been wrong about yourself or someone else before? When was the last time you ignored details that should have gone into your story and refused to insert them? That usually does not end well.

All this is heightened by the fact that you love story, you incorporate story all the time, and you are . . . wait for it . . . you are in a Story. Stories resonate with us because we are each in a Story. And this Story you are in is much bigger than the little ones you are composing in your head.

But what happens to us if we believe a false narrative? What happens when we believe something much smaller than who we really are and that lie names us and determines our identity and how we interpret life?

All this is important stuff. If we utilize story all the time in everything we do, it would probably be good to know the very components of what we use.

What does that look like?

The Components of Story

With the help of *Merriam-Webster* and a little adjusting on my part to fit our purposes, here are some common storytelling definitions to work with:

- Author—the writer, originator, creator of something.
- Point of View (POV)—a perspective from which something is viewed.
- Narrator—one who tells a story.
- Unreliable Narrator—a person/character telling a story, and the reader, or viewer of the story, cannot fully trust the person/character is telling the story accurately.
- Protagonist—the main character.
- Antagonist—the main character who opposes the protagonist.
- Inciting Incident—an event usually near the beginning that propels the protagonist out of their equilibrium and into the protagonist's desire, need, and purpose in the story.
- Character Arc—how a character's internal beliefs change or do not change over the course of a story.
- Story Arc—how a part of a story changes from one point or theme to a different point or theme.
- Climax—the highest emotional or event point of the story.
- Resolution—the main points of contention are resolved.
- Editor—one who changes, refines, and/or revises the telling of a story.
- Plagiarism—stealing a story or ideas from another to claim as your own.

How does all this work together in our lives?

It is time for me to be even more transparent with stupid things I have done. Step into some case studies on how Story has worked in my life, because I suspect that my Story is also your Story.

Prayer

Converse with the Lord about how you have followed your own story versus His Story for you.

> *Lord,*
>
> *How You have been patient with me. How You have been gracious and merciful with me when I have followed stories that have pulled me further from You. Show me Your Story and who You are and how I fit. I know You have great plans for me.*
>
> *Amen.*

Questions

- What are some of your favorite stories/movies/books?
- How did they impact you?
- How do you use the principles of story on a moment-by-moment basis?
- Are your stories about yourself and others always accurate?
- Can you name some ways that show you are living in a story?

CHAPTER 11

His Story Is Always Better Than Mine

L et's do some case studies on how I used story in the past without even realizing it. I hope you can see yourself and how you use these same components in everyday life situations as well.

Work, Fear, Love

As much as I enjoy working with people and seeing them get better, my job, like yours and every other job, can be a grind. How often do you go to work when you would prefer to do something else? How often does your job's biggest challenge include working with challenging personalities? Is there an employer out there who has decided to give their employees *more* time to do their work?

The majority of times I am working, I am thankful that God had led me to get good training to help the hurting world I see. What an honor and privilege. And the vast majority of patients are so thankful to have someone listen to them and to help them. That is when I am where I was created to be.

When I lose focus of the larger Story than mine and concentrate on me and my little story, I struggle with the grind of working with sometimes challenging situations and personalities. Anyone who works with the general public may agree that they sometimes see the best and worst of humanity. Sometimes challenging personalities are magnified because I am working with people in pain, and it is not easy to be happy and full of joy when you are in pain.

More than once I have been at my desk and looking through the medical chart of a new evaluation I am about to start. The vast majority of patients will get better with therapy. But imagine I am looking at the chart of someone in that 10 percent with a long history of a challenging physical problem that I know I probably cannot help in a significant way. And then I find out that it is not just one challenging orthopedic problem but three additional body parts I need to evaluate in the short amount of time allotted for only one body part. And the patient may be frustrated with the medical group I work with because of delays and difficulties in getting treatment, and they sometimes take out their frustration on me because I work in the medical group they are frustrated with. I can almost hear myself groan before I enter the room.

One particular time I asked God to help me with my attitude.

I walked into the room, and as I asked the young man questions, the answer to my prayer progressively took hold. My eyes and ears and heart opened. I saw him in a new way. I heard his pain and how it was changing his life. Suddenly he was a husband, a father, somebody's son, out of work trying to get through another day full of pain. My eyes watered. My heart was sensitized. I sensed God whisper in my mind, "*This* is why you are here."

Ow.

So beautiful.

So beautifully freeing.

The love and truth of God encapsulated in one simple sentence.

It wasn't about me after all.

It was about the person in pain before me.

Below is how I utilized the components of story we learned in the last chapter and how I walked into the treatment room with a less-than-perfect attitude.

Inaccurate Story 1

- Author? I composed a story in my head and made myself a victim and tried to justify my woes.
- POV? I did not see the larger Story and assumed my own POV above others in my smaller story.
- Narrator? I placed my story narrative above others' stories.
- Unreliable Narrator? That would be me. Influenced by my own selfishness, I narrated a false narrative in my head.
- Protagonist? I was the hero and main character.
- Antagonist? I made the one I am paid to serve into the antagonist.
- Character Arc? I made the patient into someone who was in pain and would always be in pain, when I did not know that as a fact.
- Story Arc? I made my story into one where I wanted to heal the world and was now bogged down, which impeded the happy ending to my story.
- Climax? I would finish what I had to do and then move on.
- Resolution? I would try to heal the rest of the world.

In my weak human power, I could not live out what I was supposed to do in the Story. Only God empowering me to move where I needed to move was my only hope. If I would have truly understood the principles of Story, this is how it should have been:

The More Accurate Story 1

- Author? God is the Author. It is His Story and not mine.
- POV? God reveals truth through His eyes and through His POV to reveal the pain in the greater Story.

- Narrator? God's voice through Scripture is the only one I can truly trust above all others. He impressed upon me who is the ultimate reliable narrator.
- Unreliable Narrator? I cannot fully trust what I see and feel. I am unreliable in my storytelling at times because of my flaws and struggles, and I need help to trust the only reliable narrator.
- Protagonist? God is the hero and main character in His Story. He wanted me to put the patient as a protagonist above my own narrative, to utilize what He trained me for—to help others.
- Antagonist? Satan is the main antagonist influencing me to take my eyes off God and His desires. But it was by my choice that I was the antagonist to what God wanted to accomplish.
- Character Arc? In God's perfect desire, the patient was to move from pain to healing. I was to move from self-centeredness to allowing God to move through me to help someone else move better in improved strength.
- Story Arc? God rules and reigns and will move people from broken to healing those whom He desires and when He desires. He desires all to be healed.
- Climax? God desires us to see His role for us and to be free. Self-limiting storytelling limits our ability to see things as they truly are.
- Resolution? To love. To serve. We are to love and to serve Him to heal others.

Story

As I mentioned earlier, I believed early in my life that I was going to die at a young age in a war. The more generalized fear of death morphed into a fear of any physical ailment that could soon turn into something more deadly or disabling.

In my twenties I feared that I had multiple sclerosis (MS). Studying about it in physical therapy school and learning the symptoms convinced me that I had MS. I had numbness and tingling in my arms and legs, along with progressive weakness. Concerning. It affected how I lived and how I was supposed to live out my future.

I fell in love with the love of my life, and I wondered if I should propose to her and whether I should get married. My symptoms were progressing, and I did not want to burden a future wife with having to care for me if it turned bad—though I knew there are many diagnosed with MS who continue to live their lives with their symptoms at bay. New medications have helped many with MS.

I second-guessed any future decisions, including buying a condo with stairs, assuming the worst was coming. But then my symptoms stabilized. I received prayer for healing several times, and though I was not fully healed in the moment, the prayers over time stabilized and stopped the progression of symptoms.

One of the last times I requested prayer for my symptoms, the person praying for me had the most unusual response. He sensed that God told him to tell me not to seek prayers for healing. I had the strange sense of confirmation of that same thought as I sensed God would do what He wanted to do with the symptoms. He was teaching me something I needed to know and grow in.

Over the years fear still, to varying degrees, compromised my mental/emotional confidence and faith. For years I did not want any MRI type of testing that would have revealed the truth one way or another, for if I avoided conclusive testing, then that would mean I still had a chance of not having it. That is how fear influenced my thinking. What crazy logic, when I could have just confronted the possibilities with courage and had the testing to finally settle the matter. Sometimes we do strange things under the influence of unnecessary fear.

After years of spiritual atrophy and loss of freedom of movement with the threat of MS looming over me, I somehow found the movement and strength to get the MRI once and for all. I would finally confront the truth.

The MRI came back negative for MS, and they never figured out why I was having symptoms. I had wasted years of unnecessary time and energy of stress and anxiety worrying about the looming threat of MS. Even if I had MS, it would not have necessarily led to the doom and gloom I feared.

What was I thinking?

I can tell you what I was thinking. I will break it down with the components of story before I got the MRI.

Inaccurate Story 2

- Author? I assumed authorship and composed a story of death and physical ailments without the faith that God was in control no matter what. Fear composed my false story with my permission.
- POV? Manipulated by fear and my perceived need for control, I assumed the role of the main POV.
- Narrator? I told the story in my head based on my fears and concerns.
- Unreliable Narrator? That would be me. I listened to fear above just getting tested. I was unreliable in my thinking and storytelling.
- Protagonist? I made myself the protagonist by protecting myself from possible bad news. Or you could say, I made

fear the protagonist. It dominated my outlook for my health.

- Antagonist? Truth. I made the truth something to avoid, as I feared I would lose control and protection in my narrative.
- Character Arc? I believed I would go from being a fully functional person to one day being in a wheelchair and unable to care for myself.
- Story Arc? I was arcing my story from healthy to soon-to-be disabled.
- Climax? I got a negative MRI result.
- Resolution? The fear of MS disappeared and I was freed of the fear of MS.

This is how my health and MS story should have gone:

The More Accurate Story 2

- Author? God is the Author of my story whether I have MS or not. God gives me the liberty to move toward or away from Him, and I should choose Him above fear, regardless of my *temporary* circumstances.
- POV? I finally asked God to reveal how I should see my situation. It is His ultimate POV over my own.
- Narrator? God is the *only* reliable narrator.
- Unreliable Narrator? I am at times an unreliable narrator, and my lack of reliability is magnified by unchecked emotions and beliefs.
- Protagonist? God is the protagonist in the Story—not me, not fear, not Satan using fear.
- Antagonist? Satan and fear turned me into my own enemy.
- Character Arc? I will grow from the fear of death to

knowing that with any illness or ailment, I will be healed. Only the timing of my healing is in question. I will be healed before I am fully with Him or when I am fully with Him. Either way, *I will be healed.*

- Story Arc? My Story regarding MS moved from being stuck in the web of my scar tissue of fear to moving more freely toward the next challenge to who I am.
- Climax? I will one day be with my Author and Great Physician, fully able to love, fully knowing I am loved, fully healed, and fully free.
- Resolution? No matter what happens, in the end God wins. Therefore, I win.

Story

So far I have mentioned how I lived the story components regarding work and health. What is most important in life? Oh, I don't know. How about *love and relationships with God above all?* That might be important!

When my wife and I were dating, we talked about our different faith journeys. We came from different backgrounds. We did not settle any differences at the time, but at least we brought them into the light of day. But when we got engaged, we had to address our differences.

I am a strong believer in family. I was raised Catholic, and I believed it was important for me to remain a Catholic for family tradition's sake. Claire was going to a Baptist church at the time. We alternated attending each other's churches, but things were still unresolved. I played with the idea of me going to my church and Claire going to her church every Sunday. Then we could meet for lunch somewhere.

Claire did not think that was a good idea. She thought we should go to church together.

Here is how I saw the situation, and this is what we did.

Inaccurate Story 3

- Author? Though we usually make joint decisions on important matters, we both thought I should take the lead. So I made myself the author above God for deciding our church situation.
- POV? I took on the role of primary POV. We would go to our separate churches and then get together after church.
- Narrator? I narrated a tale in my head that it was best to worship God separately as a couple.
- Unreliable Narrator? I was young and immature, and I trusted my own way of balancing family tradition, God, and us having separate spiritual journeys. Going to our separate churches was the best compromise.
- Protagonist? I was the main person to decide on this one.
- Antagonist? If I am honest, I made Claire the antagonist, as she did not think like me.
- Character Arc? I was moving from being afraid of death and illness to being strong in making an important decision for the health and life of our relationship . . . and stay true to family tradition.
- Story Arc? We were moving from being anxious about whether we could make it as a couple to learning more about God separately at different churches.
- Climax? We were going to learn that Charlie was right . . . again!
- Resolution? Charlie's confidence would increase, and he could be trusted to make important future decisions.

Well, how do you think that worked out? I am a bit embarrassed to tell you about this, as I was young and naive. That is a good excuse, right?

Sometimes one person is a Christ follower and the other is not, so one goes to church and the other does not. That is a challenging situation that I am sure the churchgoing one would love to see resolved. And I know there are cases where two married Christians have to go to separate churches. I am guessing that would not be God's perfect desire? But the reality is that it happens. But in this case, both Claire and I going to our separate churches was not the right choice for us as a couple. Perhaps it could work under different circumstances and with a different couple?

Eventually Claire exercised great wisdom and thought we should choose a nondenominational church that we could attend together. We were to start anew together. This is how the story components then looked:

The More Accurate Story 3

- Author? God is the Author. I play a role, but it is not my Story.
- POV? God has the best POV (imagine that!) in how we should grow together as a couple in a church, without our own personal ties and traditions attempting to impede His will. He desired us to start our new Story together.
- Narrator? God was the superior narrator to decide how Claire and I should worship Him together.
- Unreliable Narrator? The fact that we changed direction and ended up in a much better solution proved that I was not a reliable narrator.
- Protagonist? I needed to get my Story straight. When

Claire and I each put God as the protagonist above our own imperfect wisdom, our own ideas, we were then united in the same goal of placing God above our own ways. That is true unity.

- Antagonist? I had made Claire the antagonist because she had a differing opinion than mine. Perhaps examining the lineup of possible antagonist suspects, I would stand out as the primary suspect, but hiding behind me, the real antagonist desired to divide us from the start.
- Character Arc? I grew from thinking I always had the best idea to submitting to what our God thought. And sometimes God can use another to set me straight.
- Story Arc? Our Story as a couple moved from each individual doing what they thought was right to together doing what is right in the eyes of God. We are still growing!
- Climax? Claire and I grew closer together, worshipping our God together.
- Resolution? We try to follow (most of the time!) what God desires, and it set the tone for how we would live and raise our kids (most of the time!).

So let's look at our updated diagram 5 and summarize where we are now.

On the diagram you can see the heading above you: "It Always Comes Back to Story." There you are at the bottom, raising your hands up. And you are not alone. There is an adversary who will resist you in all your attempts to walk with the power and strength of the Creator over creation.

The Movement and Strength Analysis above you describes where you are moving and where you seek your strength. Are you walking toward creation as your god or toward the Creator God, who uses His creation for your benefit?

It Always Comes Back to Story

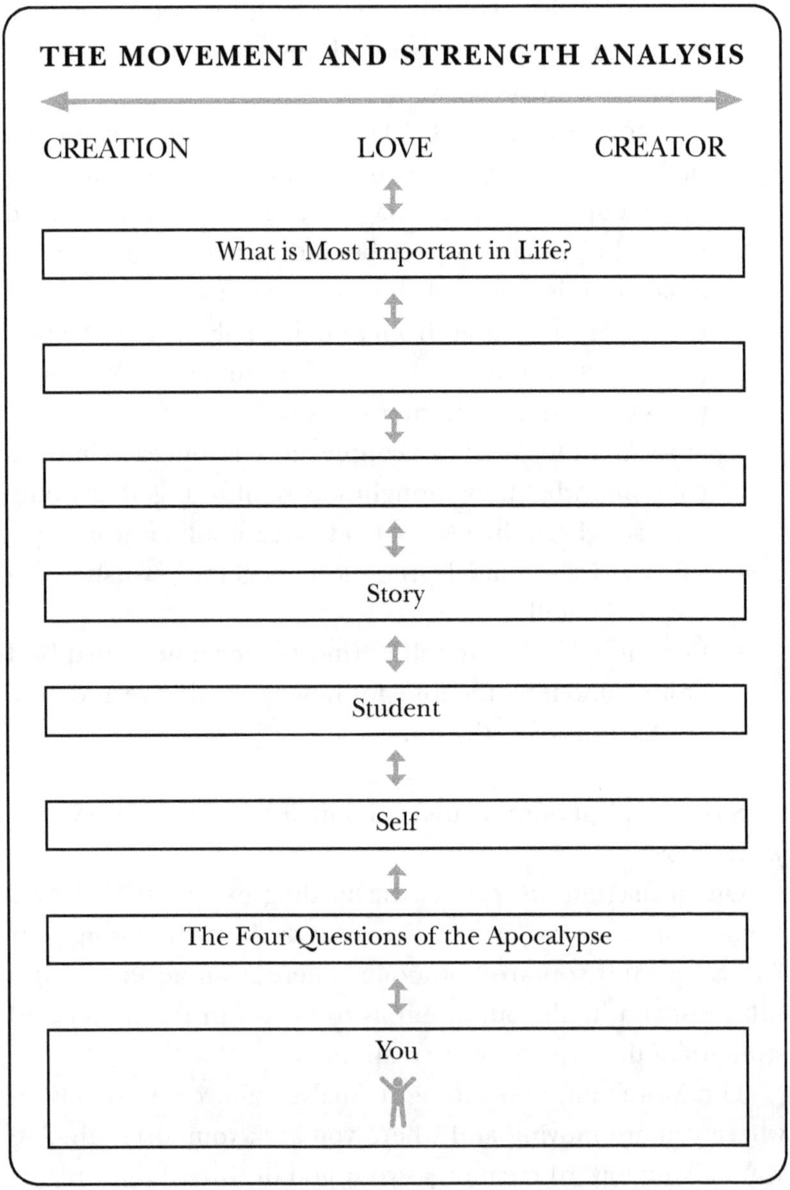

THE MOVEMENT AND STRENGTH ANALYSIS

CREATION   LOVE   CREATOR

What is Most Important in Life?

Story

Student

Self

The Four Questions of the Apocalypse

You

Diagram 5

We are all trending in one direction more than the other. We each have our mixes and combos, where we are miserable trying to please both Creator and creation. When considering my beliefs and movement in things such as morality, politics, faith, education, relationships, sex, and work, am I walking with God in some degree of liberty and strength in some arenas but challenged in others?

I will tell you that if you are anything like me, even one arena not given to God will affect your walk in other arenas. But despite the setbacks, and the two-mindedness we each have, where is your heart and mind trending overall in allegiance?

We wrestle with the Four Questions of the Apocalypse, and we hopefully grow past ourselves as individuals living the self-centered life. We hope to live as a student of life in humility, testing our beliefs as we put everything into story in our heads so we understand and navigate as we move in movement and strength.

The Power Core of Four

If I had to narrow down all the different components of story, I would do it the following way.

- Author
- Main POV
- Main Editor
- Plagiarizing

In issues as relevant as the sexual-relationship arena—pornography and premarital and extramarital sex—who is the ultimate author, main POV, and editor, and am I plagiarizing parts of His Story to conveniently create my own? For example, I have taken a truth, "God is love," and plagiarized God's truth to then create my own story (God loves me and wants me to be happy) to rationalize viewing things I know I should have not been viewing.

If you are anything like me, you have some serious skills in taking the role of author and adopting your POV as the main POV while editing and plagiarizing God's Story to rationalize just about anything we desire.

Man, we think we are so good.

But can we get our Story straight?

Prayer

Lord,

I confess I have tried to hijack Your Story and remake it into my own. I have played the role of the convenient author, main POV, and editor, and I have conveniently plagiarized Your words and intents and conveniently fashioned them as my own, with no due reverence to my Author.

Forgive my self-centered ways, and I turn away from my little lying story.

I choose to follow the Author of my faith.

Show me how.

Amen.

Questions

- What examples can you give of how you have attempted to hijack God's Story and tried to make it your own?
- Where do you struggle with getting the components of Story right, with God ruling over your relationships? With your work? Health? Money? Your beliefs about God?
- Can you give an example of how you have plagiarized God's words?

CHAPTER 12
My Story if I Am Honest

There is a resistance opposing us when we seek what is good in all arenas in life—like trying to eat healthy, exercise, and budget finances.

How about the valuable commodity of our time. Any writer will tell you that if you want to build tension in a story, use a ticking-clock strategy to ramp things up. Perhaps it could be a literal ticking clock, such as a bomb that will soon explode. Or maybe a character's life will change at a certain future moment and specific events must occur before then. Or maybe a character is slowly dying.

Perhaps a few stories come to mind. Characters needing to destroy a ring before it is too late. Trying to save a soldier during World War II before he is killed like his brothers. How about trying to destroy the ultimate weapon that can wipe out a planet? I am sure you can think of other examples in some of your favorite movies or novels.

As I get older, I am more cognizant of my own ticking clock. We each have a certain amount of time in our life bank, and we really don't know how much is left and available for us to make transactions with. If you think about it, we withdraw funds all the time through choices we make. Decisions like smoking five packs of cigarettes a day withdraws time we have left. Withholding forgiveness because of a previous spirit injury takes out time with its toll on us mentally, physically, and spiritually. Living a promiscuous lifestyle withdraws time funds. The fear of seeing the doctor and ignoring symptoms when you know something is wrong could affect remaining time. The fall of Adam and Eve in the garden affected the time funds we have today.

When you hit your thirties, then forties, then fifties and beyond, you become more aware that your time is limited here on earth. But what if I still want to spend time with family and friends, heal people, write great stories, travel? I want my loved ones to see God for who He is, and I will do everything I can with my role here in whatever time I have left. I would even spend thousands of hours of my time writing books to do exactly that.

Not only do we have a ticking clock on our lives, but in our culture we spends millions of dollars each day to numb ourselves to the reality of our ticking clocks.

Did those who struggle with addiction to unhealthy appetites wake up one day intending to become addicted to things such as drugs, hard-core or soft-core pornography, social media, shopping online, news that supports one viewpoint, toxic TV shows and movies? The algorithms with social media and your internet-related searches make you almost utterly defenseless against putting your phone down or stopping the clicks on your computer. See the documentary *The Social Dilemma* made a few years ago.[13] You have little to no chance of fully resisting the theft of your time. But yet we are each individually responsible for our choices.

We will waste much time with our varying levels of addictions and corresponding spirit injuries. Even after all my years, visual images can still pull at me from my past days leashed to pornography. Back in the days within the peak of my slavery, after giving away my choice and power, what chance did I really ever have? But I was still accountable for my choices.

---

[13] "The Social Dilemma," directed by Jeff Orlowski (2020, Netflix Original).

There can be an emotional toll to pay with how we spend our time. Either you are personally struggling with, or you know someone struggling with, fear, anxiety, insomnia, phobias, addiction, thoughts of suicide, and loneliness. What chance do we have in our own power and freedom of movement to move in freedom and strength, with the top half of our hourglass emptying every moment?

The Algorithm That Feeds My Story

A while back I had an experience in which whenever I went to an online video sharing platform, it would start a random video with autoplay. The platform's algorithm had assigned certain videos for me that would start playing, and some of them shocked me. I did not know that those types of videos would be allowed on the platform, since children could also watch that same content.

The videos would play, and in my surprise at what I saw, I had challenges pulling my eyes away. After viewing a handful of videos, the algorithm soon got me. I was stuck. I could not turn off the digital treadmill as my eyes and my mind ran with the images.

I tried to stop the visual treadmill by watching more appropriate images. But the inappropriate images came back, with then more shocking images. When I came to, I tried searching for more appropriate videos, but the algorithm would not have any of it. I was stuck and I could not turn it off.

This is how our brain works with toxic thoughts.

Our mind defaults to an autoplay story mode in each of our mind movies, and we are limited in movement by previous sins and wounds and scars of our spirit to change the autoplay of the algorithm in our head and heart. And our time meter is running. Our clock is ticking.

Here are some possible one-liners from our autoplay mind movies:

- God could never forgive me because of what I have done.
- ________________ does not love me.
- I am surrounded by idiots. Why is __________ such an idiot?
- I hate ________________
- I am such a loser. I hate myself.
- I am so ugly.
- I am so fat.
- Why am I so stupid?
- I'm too dumb.
- I have no significance.
- I have no meaning in my life.
- No one will ever love me.
- I need to do __________ to make people like and respect me.
- I mean nothing to ____________.
- I am so far above and better than ________________.
- Something bad is going to happen to me. I deserve it.
- My life story is so boring.
- I am not enough.

My Story if I Am Honest

If it always comes back to Story, I am going to present a composite story combining parts from others I have known, as well as a few parts of my own tale. This could summarize where I was and where I could be today, if left unchecked. Perhaps some of the following details are part of yours?

Where do I start? This exercise of briefly writing my story is a complete waste of time if I am not honest with you and myself. I apologize if it is a bit raw.

My whole life, I have always thought I was on my own. My dad escaped our house and never returned. Mom worked two jobs, and to her credit she never permanently left us. But she did escape within the house with her self-medicating ways.

I grew up thinking I was the infectious illness that caused my father to flee and forced mom to numb herself. I found out that just about every other person I knew was also self-treating their various injuries.

I have many wounds, but I have one wound. How could a grown adult think it was okay to do to me what he did to me? That was not okay. Someone hurting then hurt me. I had my injuries from life and the scar tissue from the internal cuts from sin upon my spirit, and like an octopus sucking me down an ocean whirlpool, it further entangled my limited movement and pulled me down into the lower depths with my meaningful relationships.

I used people to medicate me. I used things to medicate me.

I have family members who have some serious health problems. Some got cancer and heart problems and eventually died. Anxiety and fears have really hit a lot of us these last few years.

So I keep my guard up for protection. If I let some of my walls go down and I allow myself to be away from my screens, I know I have some of all of this messed-up stuff in me too. But I am different. I will be different. I have to be different, for I am the author of my own story. I am the protagonist, and my antagonists number in many as they oppose what I think is right. I can only trust myself, as others will always eventually fail me. I have to trust my heart, and only my heart.

I have been thinking about those four questions.

Why am I alive? I honestly don't know how to answer this question.

What do I live for? I like to sleep a lot. Sometimes doing my art makes me happy.

Who do I live for? All I can do is try to do what I think is best.

What is most important in life? To be happy. I am trying.

Sometimes I believe in God and that He wants the best for me. But if I am honest, I don't think He really knows what I am going through, because if He did, He would help me to get what I want.

Like a career lawmaker in DC, God does not really know what happens at the street level anymore. He is not here to see and experience how messed up things are. He is mute for what is right. He is powerless to fix things. But I do believe He is asleep somewhere in some remote location.

I am sure I am supposed to say that God is most important in life, but I do not know if there is a God, when so many people are alone, hurting, and just trying to figure things out. It seems that God would make Himself visible in some way to make us believe. I would believe if He just showed up. Walked with us. I just do not see that.

But if I am honest, I do think there has to be something out there. There has to be some way of fixing what is broken. Maybe I am just dreaming.

People don't understand the POV that I have, and if they did, they would understand that I know better than most people. People all around me are messed up. They need me to tell them what is messed up and how to fix it. But I am too busy to always be trying to edit the mess out of others' lives and their negative effects on my life. Their problems eventually affect me. It takes a lot of time and energy, and I am often tired and want to rest from everyone's drama. I could use rest.

Maybe this is all part of the journey. We are all stumbling and staggering together and trying to move toward happiness.

I have dreams, and my goal in life is to be happy, and I am here to try and make other people happy. But I have to make my dreams come true. I just have to believe in myself and keep on believing that I can make my dreams come true.

I can only do this by listening to my heart and following what I feel is right. I have to be true to myself.

I just want to be happy, and then I can die.

The clock is ticking, and the entire system seems rigged to teach and train us to be an unreliable narrator with a false identity while paralyzed in our web of scar tissue from all our war wounds, entangling us even as we wish we could liberate ourselves.

How did we get here?

How do we break free?

Prayer

Lord,

Show me the repeating algorithms that play in my head. Show me how they affect what I believe and how I live. Author of my faith, edit out what You want to edit. Show me Your Story and how I fit. I want a new Story.

Free me.

Amen.

Questions

- Do you struggle with an awareness of your ticking clock?
- How does that look?
- What does God want to do with your remaining time?
- What autoplay of thoughts replay in your mind?
- What are some one-liners from autoplay in your mind movies?
- What would God-autoplay look and sound like?

CHAPTER 13

The Most Important Sentence in History

I have my broken autobiography and you have yours. Is that all we have, and is that all there is in life?

It is time to get our Story straight.

You know your story. You saw a composite of mine and others' in the last chapter. God has His. With a multifaceted meta-narrative (His Story with infinite layers and levels), what would be a good angle to understand God communicating with us through His Word?

I'm going to cover an angle to God's Story, our Story, that is different than most.

Where do you start the Epic above all epics?

Start at the Beginning

"In the beginning God created the heavens and the earth"
(Gen 1:1 NASB).

Let's revisit some of the impact and ramifications of this simple, and most complex, first sentence we covered earlier.

- There was a beginning to time and creation.
- God preexisted before creation, and He created every-thing from nothing.
- There are multiple realms: the material and the immate-rial, the natural and the spiritual.

There is a God who created everything from nothing. There is the material realm, the components of heavens and the earth, and the immaterial, God, and later we find out about created spirit beings. There is a natural and a supernatural realm. There is the physical and the spiritual.

There is a lot to this first sentence. Reread it again. Pause and reflect. As a writer I subscribe to the belief that the first and last lines in a novel or movie are often the most important in that particular story, with the first line perhaps the most important.

I am convinced that the meaning of these first words of the Bible could perhaps be an entire book or college class in itself. There is so much packed into this brilliant first shot across the bow of every person's view of the world. I would argue that this is the most important sentence ever communicated. Let's break it down.

Read that verse one more time. But this time, pause and reflect on each individual word before you move to the next word. Done? Now read it once again and see how each word connects.

There was a beginning.

There is a God.

God created.

Everything.

What else is hidden to be revealed in this sentence?

Bigger Than Us

Have you ever suspected that there is something beyond you? Something bigger than you? The answer is in the first verse.

There it is staring at us hidden in plain sight: God claims that He had already existed before the beginning as we know it. God had to have existed before the beginning of time and creation, as God must be able to exist outside of time and creation in order to create time and creation.

Think about that.

Someone exists beyond our realm of existence. As Chuck Missler used to say, someone is communicating with us from "outside our time domain."[14]

That claim instantly has my attention.

The Meta-Classification System

Whether you and I realize it or not, we navigate and make sense of our world by classifying everything. Even if one was to deny that we classify everything, one is actually classifying just by saying they are not classifying.

How? At any given moment, we classify life into categories like truth, lie, things that we like or don't like. Good and bad. Beautiful and ugly. Pleasurable and non-pleasurable. Tastes good and does not taste good. Expensive and not expensive. Every decision I can think of that we make on a moment-to-moment basis is classified into categories that help us navigate life. You get the idea. Yes, there are many things that fall in between some extremes, but we still use a classification system to find varying degrees in between.

In physical therapy, as a McKenzie-trained PT, after evaluation and testing, we classify the patient and their particular diagnosis/injury, and then we treat accordingly. Placing a patient into the wrong category will likely yield less-than-favorable results. Sometimes treating a patient with the wrong treatment options can actually make a patient worse. Studies have shown

---

[14] Chuck Missler, "A Message from Outside Time," Koinonia House, June 1, 2013, https://www.khouse.org/personal_update/articles/2013/message-outside-time.

that the proper classification of patients' symptoms greatly improves our chances of success. We may have to adjust our initial classification as the status of the patient changes, but this classification sets us in motion to evaluate, assess, reassess, and treat appropriately.

How about everyday life outside of physical therapy? With the categories of truth and lies, if I mis-categorize, I will likely have poor results. For example, suppose I dismiss a hard truth from a trusted friend and conveniently classify that friend as mistaken or, even worse, a liar. In that case I may miss out on growing from my friend's hard truth, done in the name of love.

If I accept my own internal subjective sense that a total stranger's car should conveniently be mine and I forcibly steal it from him, I have mis-categorized truth.

If I take my temperature and it is 104.0 degrees Fahrenheit and categorize that number as not being a fever, I have misclassified fever.

Does God have a meta-classification system? Has God revealed to us His classification system for us to use? Is there a classification system that is above all other classification systems?

From the first verse in His communication to us, God reveals His classification system! And if God has a classification system, then it might be a good idea to take note.

Ready for it?

Here it is: Creator. Creation.

There is a Creator and there is His creation. That is it. It is that simple. The meta-classification of everything above all other classification systems.

Creator.

Creation.

What is the meaning of life? Whose standard shall we live by? Who is the author of all creation, the moral law, love, rebellion, good, evil? Everything fits into one of the categories in the ultimate classification system. How we classify greatly influences where we are moving on the Movement and Strength Analysis scale.

Catch your breath, because there is even more packed into this one sentence.

God's Favorite Language

According to the Ethnologue, there are over seven thousand languages still being used today (spoken or signed).[15] If there is a God, and God has something to say, which of these languages is His favorite to communicate with us? Does God even have a favorite language?

Let's back up a little bit. What does the first sentence in the Bible remind you of? The first verse is a great teaser for an epic Story ahead. There is no other more famous first line than Genesis 1:1, through all the generations.

And if the first line is a hint of an Epic to come in the succeeding pages, is this not a hint of God's favorite language in that first sentence? God's favorite language, His love language to us, is the language of Story. So much so that our love of story is knitted into us in *everything* we do. He is the Master Storyteller, and He loves to share His craft with us. We all engage, and utilize, and copy His Story skills in our everyday tales.

I would even say this is a reason for the existence of God and that His Story is further evidence of His communication to us. There is no other story that has done this like the Bible and had more influence on humanity.

---

[15] "How Many Languages Are There in the World?," Ethnologue, accessed August 25, 2025, https://www.ethnologue.com/insights/how-many-languages/.

But there is even more in this first verse than God's favorite language.

Two Stories, but One

As a fiction writer, one of the first decisions I make is what main POV I will tell the story through. I would argue that God, our Author, in the ultimate true Story, presents two possible POVs in His first sentence to us. Do you see it?

Here we go again.

Creator.

Creation.

Just like our ultimate classification system. But through the lenses of story, we can now see there are two main POVs embedded in the unfolding Epic. Life through the eyes of the Creator and life through the eyes of His creation. Do you think that had any influence on the idea of a Movement and Strength Analysis?

The outline of the entire Story is hidden in the first sentence, containing a beginning, conflict, climax, and resolution.

Do you see, encoded if you will, hiding in plain sight, a narrative teaser with the elements of a great Story in that first sentence? Do you see an outline of a beginning, middle, and end? Do you see a calm equilibrium, conflict, climax, and resolution of a great and coming dramatic tension in Genesis 1:1?

If there are two main POVs introduced with the first sentence, it is easy to conclude that at some point there will be conflict that will arise between creation and Creator.

I would propose to you that in Genesis 1:1, there is a foreshadowing of the main characters', Creator and creation, coming conflict between the two, and a climax and resolution to the conflict hidden and coded in plain sight in the same first sentence. (More on that later.)

Eventually life seen through those two different POVs in some ways becomes two different stories. In His classification system, God is God and creation is not, so truth be told, it is more accurate to say there is one true and authentic Story and one counterfeit version with an almost infinite number of sub-stories.

In my writings you will see me refer to the existence of two stories to help clarify certain points, but I acknowledge that there is really only one true Story and one main POV superseding all others. Two stories, but one.

This first sentence in the Bible is pregnant with hints of a coming Story, the main characters, the drama, and the tension of conflict, and it even has the climax and resolution all hidden inside right before our eyes.

My story is broken. So is yours.

But there is hope, as Someone coded in plain sight life-changing perspectives far greater than your own.

So what is the Story?

Prayer

Lord,

You know I love a great story. I know there is something bigger than this life. Bigger than my story. Show me more. Show me more of what is bigger than me. Bigger than my imagination. Show me how an Epic Story points to an even more Epic Author.

All in Jesus's name,

Amen.

Questions

- Can you think of another single sentence that has impacted the world more than the first sentence in the Bible?
- Can you name books that would rival the influence of the Bible?
- If there is a God, what would you expect from a God-composed Story?
- Have you ever communicated with the Author and experienced His presence while reading His Story? Can you tell a story of when this happened?
- Do you have a role in this Story?

CHAPTER 14

A Glimpse into the Epic

You could spend a lifetime just studying one single book of the Bible, let alone trying to spend your life studying the entire Bible. (I know someone who continually studies the book of Daniel. If you already know some of the crazy layers in that book, you would spend the rest of your life studying that book as well.)

There are so many different angles and facets to the beautiful gem of the Bible, from which I will try to choose one main theme. I hope I am successful presenting the Story through the two main POVs.

Creator.

Creation.

Though I cannot be inside the minds of the following characters, I have done my best to understand and express possible thought patterns of those involved. I will be speculating what might have been going on within different characters' minds. There will be some degree of artistic license but based on scriptural truths.

I am also going to break the POV rules of writing, as I am trying to place you into the alternating minds of some main characters in the historical drama. I will sometimes alternate from one mind in one paragraph and then into another mind in the next paragraph. Understanding the different POVs as they interact is a powerful thing.

I will share with you some thoughts I have as a storyteller, with biblical influencers in my life, like my previous pastors,

Tim Mackie, David Jeremiah, Donald Grey Barnhouse, Chuck Missler, Ryan Pitterson, L. A. Marzulli, and podcasts like *Blurry Creatures* and *The Days of Noah*.

I hope to show you the tension between the conflicting POVs so there are some paragraphs seen through the creation POV that oppose the Creator's POV, and vice versa. Hang on tight as I alternate between Creator and creation.

We will then eventually put it all together.

Buckle up. Make sure you are securely fastened. Here we go.

The Story

"In the beginning God created the heavens and the earth."
(Gen. 1:1 NASB).

"You were in Eden, the garden of God . . . you were the anointed cherub who covers, and I placed you there. You were on the holy mountain of God . . . and you sinned; therefore I have cast you as profane from the mountain of God."
(Ezek. 28:13–16).

God created all things, including the angels and Lucifer, later to be called Satan. The Master Artist and Gardener created the garden of Eden and all the different worlds. God gave the angels authority to rule over parts of God's creation. Satan was preeminent of all the angels and was with God. He was beautiful in all ways above all that was created. Pride in his beautiful ways rooted in his heart and said, *I will make myself like God.*

He led a rebellion with other angels against God.

God separated the defectors from heaven.

Satan and his followers had rebelled against their God and His rulership. They twisted the light and the dark into their own selfish desires apart from God. The angels who chose themselves above God watched God break from His previous pattern of creation as He created a brand-new being not seen before.

The once highly esteemed angels stood in awe and fear, as the new being looked different. It acted differently. It was not like the angels.

God created a human in His own image.

Satan burned within. *God's offspring now rule over what was taken from me. Eden is mine.* God walked with His children. The footsteps of God moved in rhythm with theirs and reminded Satan of the horrific songs of worship in heaven.

Sometimes God and His humans conversed about the deep things of beauty, and sometimes they conversed with the birds and animals about the lovely things.

The Father's love emanated all around. Friendship. Relationship with each other and all creation. Beauty for the eyes and beauty for food. They could eat from any of the trees, especially the tree of life, but God told them one thing they could not do. God told them not to eat from the tree of knowledge of good and evil or they would die.

Satan studied the new beings. The intruders. The occupiers. *God loves them. They walk on my ground and have what is mine. They are created with the same free will. My free will.* He knew the only commandment God had given them. He knew about the one tree they were not to eat from. He hated God. He hated them. He loathed the ones created in the image of the God he loathed, who'd cast him out of home.

God ruled over all and created all.

How could Satan be like God after God removed him further from his desired throne?

Satan seethed within. His eyes narrowed. *They are not to eat from the tree. I will make them eat from the tree. God created these new beings in*

His image, and I will make the humans into my image, and make them rule as I desire. I must, and I will kill these lower-than-the-angels beings, who will rule over all of mine with their Father if I do not stop them.

Satan shook his head. *God should have loved the angels more than these lower beings. I despise them. They remind me of their Father. I will strike dead what God loves most.*

He entered into a proxy serpent and waited for the right moment. Now he had them in sight. They were alone.

Now the serpent was more crafty than any beast of the field which the Lord God had made. And he said to the woman, "Indeed, has God said, 'You shall not eat from any tree of the garden'?"

And the woman said to the serpent, "From the fruit of the trees of the garden we may eat; but from the fruit of the tree which is in the middle of the garden, God has said, 'You shall not eat from it or touch it, lest you die.'"

And the serpent said to the woman, "You surely shall not die! For God knows that in the day you eat from it your eyes will be opened, and you will be like God, knowing good and evil."

The same free will within Satan also dwelled within the lesser beings, the humans. Satan fixated his will to take theirs.

The man stood near the woman. She reached away from them. He did not stop her. She ate from the fruit of the tree of the knowledge of good and evil. He reached toward her. A new sensation moved upon his face as his chest moved toward and away from him in an unfamiliar way. He placed his hand on his pounding chest. His best friend. His lover. *She is dying. She is separated from our Father. She is separated from me.*

The woman tried to fix her eyes on the missing part of the fruit in her trembling hands. She turned toward him. *I have never seen that emotion in his eyes before.* She closed her eyes. *What have I done?*

The man remained standing still. *What did I do?* He tried to put his shaking hand in hers but was unable. *I cannot undo what we have done.* In addition to God's love for him, God gave him love with the woman, the only one he had truly known from God's creation. She was now essentially gone. He held the fruit in his hand. *I will never see her again.* His chest burned within. *Then we will die. Even if we are apart from Father.* He took a bite.

Something cracked. Something broke. Was it an audible break resounding throughout the garden and beyond, or was it just a loud echo emanating from inside each of them? What was this death that broke through the open door into their home? Something new now pressed within their chests. They both bent forward. What made their chests pound so hard? Why was it more difficult for their chests to rise and fall? New noises came out of their mouths and noses as they tried to breathe.

Something different broke through and coursed their bodies, as if an intruder assumed control of a new home. It pounded within everywhere. A new sensation. Pain? Was this death? Something stopped existing inside. Though the man and woman trembled and tried to hold each other, there was more distance between them. There seemed to be an invisible canyon, with each of them now standing on opposite sides.

Satan smiled and slithered. The man and woman. Abducted. Kidnapped. Human trafficking. *They are mine.*

The man and the woman gasped. Voices other than their own whispered and screamed inside their heads. *What moved into me? What is this now inside me?* Just as Satan had spoken within and through the serpent, now a singular voice above the other voices, and different from God, entered and spoke within the man and the woman.

They both dropped the fruit. Now they were naked. The Father would soon arrive for their walk. *Our hands cannot cover us!* With fumbling fingers they sewed leaves together. Their hearts both raced away and were trapped within.

They turned their heads. Footsteps in the distance. The steps seemed harder. Heavier this time. The ground trembled toward them. "Run! We must run!" They ran and hid behind the trees, with a large tree between the man and the woman. Their heaving chests united in timing.

The footsteps stopped on the other side of the trees. The all-seeing and all-knowing God asked His children, "Where are you?"

They stepped out with shaking hands over their bodies, with the half-eaten fruit lying between them and their Father.

Father was not pleased. Nor surprised. God told Satan, and the man and the woman, that as a result of their sin of disobeying their Father, there would now be enmity between Satan and the woman, between his seed and her seed. The woman's seed would one day crush the head of Satan, and Satan's seed would one day bruise the heel of the woman's seed.

In the days of innocence, the presence of our Father walked with Adam and Eve in the garden. They loved together. They walked together. They lived together. But things were different now.

Eve pondered what this seed of hers was. Was she like a plant or a tree? Would she somehow have another human spring forth from her own body? How would that happen? That had never happened before. *Can this seed of mine undo what we have done? Can this seed one day grow and make things right?*

Satan studied Adam and Eve. His lie deceived the humans into doing his own will. *I now have legal authority over them and their world. I can create many more lies and my own laws, for them to serve me. Because I have now changed creation to decay and then die, I can stop the seed of the woman from coming. My reign and my kingdom now rule.*

Satan had a strategy. And he learned the secret weakness of God, now fully exposed, that could not be covered. God had given Satan and Adam and Eve the same liberty to choose to walk with or walk away from God. And liberty becomes license to abuse liberty. What madness! *The flawed God should not be allowed to rule! Only a flawed Creator would ever allow free will and the possibility of bringing forth a curse to inflict upon all of His own beloved creation! Only limiting the movement of the inferior beings through my full control, my power, and my strength can undo what is now broken. What kind of all-powerful God would allow the possibility of rejection of God? What kind of almighty God would allow a lesser and inferior being to choose the opposite of what the all-powerful God wanted?* Now God was stuck in honoring His promise of death to His own offspring. God made a mistake allowing free will, and if God made a mistake, the pinnacle of His creation could overcome the Creator to fix that mistake by ruling with power, strength, and control over those who desired power, strength, and control. After all, they chose Satan to rule. Satan would stop the seed from crushing him. God's weakness was Satan's strength.

The disobedience of Adam and Eve caused a spiritual death, ensuring a physical death would follow. God removed Adam and Eve from His physical presence and from His garden temple. He sent His offspring away from the garden to prevent them from eating from the tree of life and perpetually remaining in their brokenness.

They were no longer home. Eve lifted her hands. *What have I done? Is the pain I will one day experience with childbirth going to be worse than the pain I feel now?*

Adam held up his hands. *What have I done?* Work was now harder. His body now suffered. Plants and trees began dying. They were now all under a different ruler and the consequences of their choice. They were now not their own and belonged to another.

Satan continued studying the humans. God does not lie. *The seed. Where is the coming seed?* Adam and Eve had two sons, Cain and Abel. Abel had a soft heart for his Father. Abel reminded him of the loathsome God. Satan raged. Was Abel the coming seed to destroy Satan? Cain rose up against his brother Abel.

Satan had brought fear and death to creation. It was now time to bring murder.

Abel's blood cried out to God as it spilled, seeped, and stained the hard ground. God heard Abel's cry. Cain protested against God's punishment of banishment as he cried out, "I will be hidden from your presence."

Satan admired the view. *The seed is now a corpse on my ground.* He'd killed two with one act. The promise of God lay lifeless, with only his blood crying out. And how could Cain, the murderer, be the seed of God to rule over Satan, when Cain allowed Satan to rule over him?

Adam and Eve brought forth Seth, and he entered the fray. They held their son. *Is this the seed that will fix what we have done? Or will he walk the same path as Cain?*

Satan could not stop Seth. But he was not the seed that would end Satan's rule. Over the years, Satan persuaded most weak humans to believe him and to reject God. *I am their one true god, and I will create my own breed of humans made in my image for my will and for spreading my kingdom. I will train them to one day believe my coming seed.* If Seth was not the seed, then could the seed come through Seth and future individuals and their bloodlines?

How can I stop the coming seed? Satan plotted. *When shall I bring forth my seed?* God had said the seed would be through the woman. It had to be purely human. Angels descended onto earth to have sexual relations with human women, and hybrid angel and human giants soon roamed and ruled the earth.

Sin spread among creation like never before. Morally and genetically corrupted hybrid humans turned against each other and humans and God.

Satan polluted humanity. Was most of humanity even human anymore? He colonized all of the human race and transformed them into his own image. Into less than human. With no pure humans, the seed from the woman, the seed from God, could not take hold. The earth, without a human seed from the woman, would soon be Satan's.

Noah walked with God. God spoke to Noah. "I myself am bringing the flood of water upon the earth, to destroy all flesh in which there is the breath of life . . . everything that is on the earth shall perish." Noah was not corrupted by Satan and the fallen angels. God called Noah and his family into the ark to save them and to preserve and save the remnant of humans from the coming judgment.

God destroyed Satan's corrupted creation under flood waters.

Noah braced himself as the ark tilted and even seemed to bend under the wrath around him. He bent his head and prayed. *I thank You God that Your seed and Your people are aboard. You saved us. You save yours.* The genetic bloodline of the seed of the woman was on board the ark and advancing.

Where is he? There was nothing Satan could do. The seed had to be aboard the ark, and he could not stop the flood waters from destroying years of preparing and executing his plan. His army of corrupted humans was drowning. He could only regroup. He set himself to infiltrate and colonize the survivors and their offspring after the flood. He continued his multi-generational grooming of the people for his coming seed, a one-world leader and a consolidation of power at Babel. God rejected Satan's efforts for a one-world government apart from

God, and He separated and dispersed the people by creating many languages.

God called Abraham to leave what he knew to start a new people in a new land. Israel formed twelve tribes, and the seed flowed through the tribe of Judah. Satan moved within Pharaoh to enslave and persecute the ancient Hebrews and kill the young boys to stop the seed.

But God was with the Israelites and protected a baby from the infanticide and hid him in a small ark floating down the Nile River. Pharaoh's daughter took him for herself. God raised up Moses in the home and empire of Pharaoh, the slave master.

Was Moses the promised one?

Moses, in the power and presence of God, freed the Israelites from slavery in Egypt and escaped with them toward the promised land. God guided them with a pillar of cloud by day and a pillar of fire by night. His presence accompanied them in a mobile tabernacle.

During their journey, the Israelites rebelled against God and Moses, so God struck them with the bites of poisonous snakes. God healed and saved their lives when those who were bitten obeyed God and looked up at a bronze snake on a pole.

I am with you. God dwelled with His people in the temple in the promised land. His glory was so great and His desire to forgive His people so grand, that only the high priest could enter the cube-shaped holy of holies in the temple to intercede for the forgiveness of the sins of the people.

Satan lied to another generation. Acceptance and compliance to Satan among the people multiplied throughout humanity. The glory of God departed the temple. The temple was destroyed by those who had believed Satan.

A prophet of God declared that a Son would be born in Bethlehem, with the government with no end resting on His shoulders on the throne of David, and He would be called Mighty God.

Satan studied his options. He moved the weapons of fear and murder into the heart of King Herod to kill the young boys around the time this Son was to be born.

Mary caressed her stomach. *Am I carrying the seed of God?* God protected Mary and Joseph and the baby growing within Mary. Powers shifted, and Someone warned Joseph and Mary in a dream to move away from the hunters. It seemed that there was no room for the seed to enter the hard ground.

Mary delivered her boy among the animals. This was not a fallen angel and human hybrid. God returned back to earth in the form of a baby, to walk with His people. He is Emanuel. God with us. Fully God. Fully human.

Satan knew the prophecies. The seed was somewhere. *Did I kill him when I killed the boys?* Though Satan was allowed to rule the earth, he raged at failing to stop the seed. Jesus grew, and Satan tempted Him in the desert. And failed. This Jesus was a new Adam. This Jesus was God. Day by day, person by person, Satan continued preparing the people for his will. He influenced people to try to kill God with us. He moved through the free will given to God's creation.

Satan influenced his willing proxies, Roman, and religious leaders and soldiers. The Son of God healed and snatched many out of Satan's grip of colonization and his kingdom. Satan could find no opening within Jesus. Satan entered the heart of one of Jesus's inner circle.

The seed stopped breathing on a cross.

The seed was dead.

Satan and his proxies celebrated. They made God a liar. God lied. The seed did not crush the head of Satan. The seed was dead! Satan still ruled. The dead seed and the dead promise was buried in a tomb of death to rot like all other previous humans, lower than angels, like in all previous generations. There was no one to save the humans, as their Savior was rotting and would be consumed by worms.

I save mine. Light and power burst through the burial cloth. Death denied. Jesus rose from the dead. He purchased the slaves with His very blood. Freedom. God does not lie. God triggered the trap and snapped the hope of Satan. It ensnared Satan in his blind rage. The Son returned to His Father, and the presence of God in the form of the Holy Spirit came to earth and indwelled not in a garden, a tabernacle, or a temple building but to His temple—but this temple was different. This temple was living. Breathing. Moving. Walking. In new strength. The seed died and seeded the church. The presence of God dwelled in the temple, and the church of believers was now His temple. Every believer was both a living temple and a living stone of the larger temple. The living stones were to move in strength for the Rock, the High Priest now within them.

Satan failed. He and his proxies' violent fury are ramping up, as he knows his remaining time on earth is short. Prophecies tell us that King Jesus will soon return to rule and reign in His millennial kingdom and then in the eternal kingdom within the New Jerusalem, which will come down to earth from heaven. The New Jerusalem will be laid out like a giant cube. The new holy of holies! Now God is the temple. The city is a temple. We will live in the city. We will live in God. God is in us, and we will live in God.

It is too late for Satan to stop the seed of the woman from being born. *I loathe Him, and I loathe those whom He loves and those He dwells within. My seed is coming.* His hate and vengeance grows. Though he cannot create from nothing like God, is it too late for him to convince others he has raised up another messiah, another savior long prophesied, his own seed? Is it too late to raise up his own hybrid army and kingdom of followers? Is it too late to eliminate you and your loved ones before the Story can be known?

God is with us.

He has always been with us.

Prayer

Pause and reflect on the Story you live in.

Lord,

Sign me up for this Epic! Deal me in! I am tired of my dead story. I acknowledge my sins and ask You for forgiveness. Forgive me. I believe, Lord Jesus, that You died for my sins. I ask You to enter into my heart, and I commit to You above all others. Show me how You want to use me in my role.

Amen.

Questions

- If you were Satan, how would you feel about being used like a tool to build your own destruction?
- God's sense of time is different than ours. Do you think that in some way in the future you will actually be able to experience each part of the Story in real time?
- What does this Story say about the Author?
- God has always been with us. How have you personally experienced His presence?
- Do you have peace or unrest about the future days?

CHAPTER 15

A Glimpse of the Epic Explained

The angle of the Story we covered last chapter is so important, it is worth reviewing, elaborating, and directing with specific verses so you can check the facts on your own. Don't blindly trust me. Check for yourself. Who God is and who you are in the grand narrative is that important.

Our Story begins with God, and His ever-present presence, creating all things (Gen. 1:1). God entrusted Satan, His preeminent angel, with authority to rule. Satan desired to be like God and rebelled and fell (Isa. 14:12–14).

Though God had allowed Satan to rule over earth for a time, two new creations now walked on his land to steward over what was once his. These new creations had authority to have dominion over earth.

God, our perfect love and preeminent relationship, lived with His children as His presence literally walked with us (Gen. 3:8). Our footsteps moved in rhythm with His in our Eden paradise. We walked freely with God.

Satan desired to retake the legal authority given to the new creatures. To execute vengeance against God and death upon the usurpers called man and woman, Satan conversed with the man and woman and utilized a partial truth (there is a God—note he never denied there is a God), then doubt (Did God really say what He said?), and then the lie (you will not die, and you can be like God and author your own story independent of God).

Satan, the original racist slave master, colonized the first two human hearts by sneaking in his racism (he hates the human race) and slavery (to ensnare through sin). He colonizes hearts for his kingdom with the lie that Adam and Eve can be like God within the Trojan horse of freedom and autonomy from a God holding out on us. And like each of us today, Adam and Eve conveniently believed (Gen. 3:6–7).

As a result of their sin, God told the man, woman, and Satan that a seed from the woman would come to crush the authority of Satan (Gen. 3:15) and that Satan's seed would bruise His heel. God removed His physical presence and removed Adam and Eve from the garden to prevent permanent brokenness.

Much of the rest of our Story consists of Satan trying to stop the seed of the woman from usurping Satan's rule and to create his own seed to usurp God.

Satan tried to stop the seed through Cain killing Abel (Gen. 4:8), through fallen angels polluting the human bloodline that could carry the seed (Gen. 6:1–6), killing the young boys to stop Moses (Ex. 1:22), influencing the Israelites to rebel against God and Moses as they traveled to the promised land, and just about every other story line running through the Old Testament.

While traveling to the promised land, God foreshadowed One who would one day be lifted up, and those who looked upon Him would be healed (Num. 21:5–9), and He would come from among them (Deut. 18:15–18).

The presence of God moved with Moses and the Israelites in the pillar of fire by night and pillar of cloud by day and lived with them in the mobile tabernacle (Ex. 25:8) as the Israelites walked to the promised land.

Later, Satan influenced the people to choose a human king over God as their King (1 Sam. 8:4–5), and Saul rose to be their king. But God appointed David to one day replace Saul, so Satan may have used Saul as a proxy and attempted to kill David to stop the line of the seed. God protected David.

With His people in the promised land, God's presence dwelled in the cube-shaped holy of holies within the temple (1 Kings 6:20, 9:3). But Satan influenced Israel to sin, and Ezekiel, in a vision, saw the glory of God departing the temple (Ezek. 10) before it was destroyed.

Satan influenced King Herod to kill the baby boys (Matt. 2:16) to stop the seed, but God protected the seed within Mary. The baby grew, and the presence of God, Jesus, returned to once again walk with His people here on earth. Satan had time, as the seed had not yet destroyed Satan's authority on earth. Satan influenced the murder of Jesus. While Jesus was on the cross, Jesus takes us on a flashback to when David was on the run for his life from Saul, to help us connect the dots of the seed dying in Psalm 22 to the seed dying on a cross in Matthew 27 (more on this later).

Jesus rose from the dead and ascended to the Father as the presence of God, in the form of the Holy Spirit, came down and dwelled within the new temple within His people on earth. Satan lost whatever legal authority he had. There was no weakness of God. It was all part of the plan. Satan rages to kill and destroy all the living temples indwelled with God. The presence of God that once walked with His people in the garden, was withdrawn, and He removed Adam and Eve from the garden because of sin but then was present within the tabernacle, the temple, and is now within His people, as His living temple walks and moves in God, with God!

I am inspired by a sermon decades ago from a pastor, Daryl Johnson, speaking about the book of Revelation. In our bright future, for there is no need for the sun or the moon, the cube-shaped New Jerusalem (Rev. 21:16), an extension of heaven coming down to earth, will be our future home. In Revelation 21 we are told that God will be the temple, the city will be the temple (the city is laid out like a cube, like the holy of holies in the previous temple), and we will live in the city.

Fix on this thought: God is within us today, and we will one day be within God within His city. Our city.

God desires to be within us so we will be within Him.

The love of God, and our relationship with Him, is what is most important in life (Luke 10:20; Ex. 20:3; Matt 7:21–27). It's God. This is where we get our love, liberty of movement, and our strength and power from.

Prayer

Lord,

You created me to live and breathe and move in You. You created my present body, soul, and spirit to live in this life, and when I gave my life to you, You created a new me to move in You when I am with You! You have already made me into a new creature, and one day I will be even more of a new creation.

Teach me. Show me how to move in You, even for today, as You prepare me for my future fully with You.

Amen.

Questions

- If God created you to live, breathe, and move in Him, how should you live?
- Are you capable of living, in your own strength and power, how God created you to be?
- Are there desires of your heart that are consistent with how God would desire you to move?
- Is this Author different than any other author? How?
- What will life in the New Jerusalem be like?

CHAPTER 16
Your Enemy's Main Strategy Against You

I t always comes back to Story.

It comes back to living the Creator's Story or somebody else's.

Which story we believe, and therefore live, is quite powerful. Transformational. The overall Story, especially highlighted in Genesis 3, exposes your opponent's game plan. The interaction between Satan and Adam and Eve in Genesis 3 documents one of the most consequential conversations ever recorded, with more ramifications than any other. It presents your opponent's playbook and strategies against you, and it defines and explains pretty much everything we encounter and live out each day.

It is worth reviewing what Satan did, because it is what he still does against you and your loved ones time after time after time, today and tomorrow. He has had no reason to change. He has one main "magic" trick, and his track record indicates that a one-trick magician/illusionist is all he needs to be. Satan executed a brilliantly effective strategy from that initial discussion with Adam and Eve, and that strategy affects you today. Let's read Genesis 3:1–5 once again and see if you can see what he did.

Now the serpent was more crafty than any beast of the field which the Lord God had made. And he said to the woman, "Indeed, has God said, 'You shall not eat from any tree of the garden'?" And the woman said to the serpent, "From the fruit of the trees of the garden we may eat; but from the fruit of the tree which is in

*the middle of the garden, God has said, 'You shall not eat from
it or touch it, lest you die.'"
And the serpent said to the woman, "You surely shall not die!
"For God knows that in the day you eat from it your eyes will be
opened, and you will be like God, knowing good and evil."
(Gen. 3:1–5)*

Did you see it?

From the long list of story components I mentioned earlier, though all are important and play a role on a moment-by-moment basis, I will bring it down to our power core of four we covered earlier. This is worth reviewing.

- Author?
- POV?
- Editor?
- Plagiarizer?

The power core of four again condenses the major components of Story. In relation to the first recorded conversation between Satan and Adam and Eve, did you see how Satan shifted things? He moved the belief of God as Author, main POV, and Editor of His own Story (God will one day edit Satan out of the Story) to Satan, behind the scenes, assuming the roles of author, main POV, editor, and plagiarizer.

He believed he could hijack the Story and remake it into his own image and tale and convince others to believe his revised narrative for their own benefit. He groomed Adam and Eve to believe the wrong story.

Satan plagiarized and perverted parts of God's Epic, the beliefs that there is a God and there is a moral law, by taking these principles and making them his own, with no due credit to the Author of those principles. He shifted the focus of the Story by deceiving the early humans into believing they could be the main author, the main POV above God, and the main editor. He plagiarized and perverted God's Story, and in the process made God the main antagonist!

In the beginning of the Story, literally the first sentence, and then fleshed out throughout the rest of the book, God is the Author, main POV, and main Editor, and He does not plagiarize, as He is the original. If someone attempts to hijack God's Epic and assume authorship with their own main POV by editing and plagiarizing God's Story into their own, God reminds us that He is the Author, life is through His main POV, and He has every right to edit out the liars and lies and call into account the plagiarizer.

Once again it was a simple satanic strategy and formula: partial truth, doubt, lie.

Update

Do you think Satan used this successful strategy only one time with Adam and Eve and then abandoned it?

Let's look at our diagram 5.

It always comes back to Story. Four questions get to the heart of who we believe we are. There we are at the bottom seeking help and direction in the Story we are in. But we have an adversary with us. He has tremendous influence on everything about us, and around us, with his strategies of partial truth, doubt, and lies.

But God is more.

Where do we place our love? Looking at the top, we are either moving more toward the Creator or creation as our ultimate God. We know that love and relationships are the most important things in life, and our love and relationship with God is the most important of all.

It Always Comes Back to Story

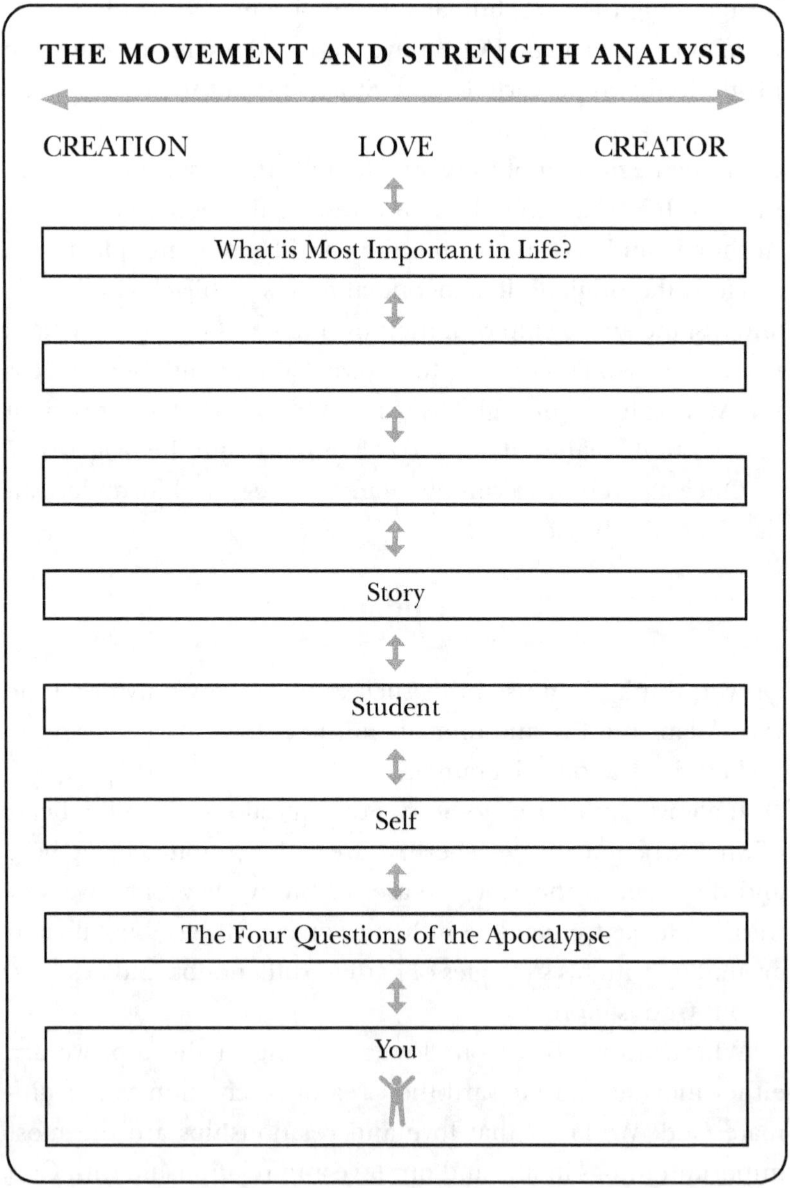

THE MOVEMENT AND STRENGTH ANALYSIS

CREATION   LOVE   CREATOR

What is Most Important in Life?

Story

Student

Self

The Four Questions of the Apocalypse

You

Diagram 5

How do we get to what is most important, our love and relationship with God, and then move more freely in love and relationship with others? We utilize different levels of truth.

The levels of truth are not always necessarily in the order on the diagram. They can move independently of and dependently with another and can be in any order at any time. I presented an order that I see often.

There is the self mode. Hopefully, we grow out of exclusive time in self mode, and we can then move into another truth mode. Student mode is where we move with humility and test everything we consider and believe. We move into Story mode at all times interchangeably with all the other modes and would be wise to use His Story to help us navigate toward what is most important in life.

These are some of the main principles we utilize at different times. But there is resistance to everything that is good for us. Our adversary knows the playbook of all our weaknesses and tendencies better than any current algorithm and AI. We conveniently believe his competing story, and we fall for it almost every time. The time-tested combination of a partial truth, doubt, and then a lie works with our convenience and permission. We are accountable.

There is a correlation between how far we have walked in one direction on the Movement and Strength Assessment scale and the effectiveness of Satan's strategy. The further we walk toward creation as our god, left unchecked, is satanic colonization. We are held responsible for our decisions. The further we walk toward the Creator as our God, the less effective Satan's strategy is, as the real King assumes His rightful reign within.

Our Cold Reality

We know there is a God and He loves us and He is all powerful. We know we are in an epic Story. But if we are honest about our own power and abilities, we don't have enough of those qualities to overcome a spiritual being created before us, operating with his many proxies with seemingly greater spiritual power, and greater intel, and greater time for learning and plotting than the best of our technologies. He has greater access to both the material and immaterial realm, and can probably guess accurately the vast majority of times what will be eventually effective against us.

Again, this is not a self-help book. We, frankly, don't have enough ability to move and utilize our own strength to get to what is most important in life and to then navigate in that. We are weak. We are stuck and locked in our own sins and bad decisions, and Satan knows our weaknesses more than we know them ourselves.

That is why we can fall short.

That is why we don't know who we truly are and why we cannot free ourselves from our abduction and false identity. That is why most people's ticking clocks run out of time before they live what is most important in life.

We are stuck.

We are rigid in our convenient and ignorant ways.

There is an unscalable gap between us and reaching what is of most importance. And like a powerless fly stuck and immobile in a sticky webwork of sin and scar tissue, we wait for the giant spider to finish us off before our remaining time is sucked out of us.

Now what do we do?

How does the Story bridge into our everyday life?

Prayer

Lord God,

I cannot fix what is broken. I fall for Satan's tricks all the time, and I usually cannot stop myself. I must confess that at times I want what Satan wants for me. I am undone! I confess my sins. I believe You died for my sins. Forgive me. Live in my heart so I can move in you. Make me that new creature that you desire. Remake me. Restore me. Lead me. Open my heart to You above all things.

In Jesus's name.

Amen.

Questions

- Can you think of a specific time you were fooled with a partial truth, doubt, and/or lie?
- Can you think of a time when you were fooled into thinking you were the ultimate main POV in a situation?
- Have you ever tried to edit God out of a situation?
- Can you think of a time when you plagiarized God's words to fit your own convenient story?
- How can you prevent yourself from being deceived by Satan?

CHAPTER 17

Level IV Truth Mode Versus Your Enemy

Earlier we did an outline tour of the Bible from the beginning to the end. From the beginning of time to our great future with God. From today's vantage point, let us flash back in our Story.

David was prophesied to be the king of Israel, and he is now on the run. Did Satan think the seed that was to come and destroy Satan's authority was David, or through his lineage?

Satan is severely limited in knowledge and power compared to God. It is likely that Satan wants to eliminate David to kill the coming seed, and to seed chaos in Israel, and to prevent Israel from being the holy ground for the coming seed to rule. Satan moved through Saul to chase down and kill David, and the shepherd boy was on the run for his life.

David, in his anguish and pain, cries out:

> *My God, my God, why hast thou forsaken me?*
> *Far from my deliverance are the words of my groaning...*
> *But I am a worm, and not a man,*
> *A reproach of men, and despised by the people.*
> (Ps. 22:1, 6)

Bible scholars over the years have taught that the term used in Hebrew for *worm* can also be translated "scarlet" or "crimson" and can be referencing a unique type of worm. Henry Morris, and others, have described this worm as a special type of scarlet worm that produced a crimson red dye that was used for dying clothes in ancient days.[16] The female worm would so firmly attach herself to wood or a tree that she could never leave. As she protected her eggs, she died and released her crimson fluid, which then covered her eggs and the surrounding wood.

So what is happening with David in this moment? I will speculate somewhat here, but I believe that Scripture hints at the possibilities. While running for his life, David had a flash-forward to the coming POV of Jesus on the cross. The presence of the coming seed dwelled within David and showed David His own death by crucifixion in the future. God was with David in his suffering. David, with his life on the line, had a flash-forward of Someone who was going to be tortured and was to die attached to the wood of a tree, and as he died, His blood would cover over His offspring. His own.

Someone inhabited David in his present time to give him a POV from Someone else in the future, which would one day be the biggest POV change of all time.

Now let us flash-forward from David's day to Jesus on the cross in his final moments of life: "My God, my God, why hast thou forsaken me?" (Matt. 27:46).

Just so you and I didn't miss it, in the moment Jesus was dying on the cross, Jesus takes us on a flashback (which I believe confirms He was with David in the past when he cried out!) and connects dots for us from Jesus back to David, to when David was having a flash-forward to Jesus, linking David and the future to Jesus on the cross!

He was with us. He is with us. He will be with us.

This is Jesus, the Savior of the world.

This is your Savior.

God.

---

[16] Henry Morris, *Biblical Basis for Modern Science* (Baker House, 1985), 73.

He chose to stick himself on a tree until death. On that day He was exalted and lifted up for us to see, and He shed His blood to cover over you, and your life, to heal you with His own blood in His death, to give you life. He is beyond our power limitations in movement and strength and time and knowledge.

You can't do this life and break through all your sins and internal scar tissue, heal yourself, and move in His full liberty and strength, to gain what is most important in life, in your own weak power. The system of Satan in this world has everything rigged against you. He has governments, most of the storytellers, most of social media, writers, journalists, schools, universities, professors, megacorporations and CEOs, Hollywood, and celebrities telling his story and speaking partial truths, doubts about God, and lies. You have no chance in your own movement, power, and strength, yet you will be held accountable for your decisions.

This reminds me of one of the most insightful, tragic, ironic, and even comical moments in Scripture. Before Jesus was murdered, Pilate asks Jesus, "What is truth?" in John 18:38.

It was standing right in front of him!

Truth is not fully found in lofty ideals, or subjective senses and feelings, or science, or college professors, or activists, or what the rich and powerful say it is.

Pilate saw it himself. Or did he?

Truth be told, truth is a person. Truth is God.

Humble yourself.

Sit at the feet of the Master Teacher.

You and I need a Savior.

Often we need to move from self mode, into student mode, into Story mode, in no particular order, and now into the Savior mode, where the Savior of the world indwells within *you*. He moves within you, with His POV above all others. And the Holy

Spirit acts like Jesus here on earth, guiding and empowering us (more on this in a future book).

You are like me, and you need to have Jesus within you, to get over yourself. To be a student in humility and testing all beliefs, immersing yourself in His Story above your own, to gain love, insight, wisdom, strength, and power to move freely with Him within you. He gives you the importance of the past, present, and future while giving you flashbacks, flash-sideways, and flash-forwards of your life in His Story, to navigate in His love and relationship.

Level Four Truth: Savior Mode

What is life like with the Savior in me and in you?

Imagine if you were living as a character before the beginning of one of your favorite movies. The story's author whispered in your ear and told you ahead of time the main scenes. In essence, the author told you a basic outline of your story, with some specifics, but left out plot twists and tension leading to the mentioned events.

Fast-forward into the future. Now you are moments away from the start of the climax of the story. You are at a crossroads and must choose between playing it safe and not growing as a character, or risking it all and leaning into the moment to grow. Would your previous additional intel from the author prepare you, gird you up, for what lies ahead for you?

Would it help you, give you more confidence, that not only does the Author know the future of His Story but that the Author also knows the POVs, and thoughts and actions, of all characters in the Story, while you are limited to just your own POV and what is immediately in front of you? And the Author of the Story you are in communicates with you in real time.

This would contrast what you already know. Truth be told, you cannot always trust what you think and feel within yourself about yourself. And about all others.

We live in interesting days. It can be challenging to understand the craziness in our lives. I have full confidence that the world will be crazier in your present time as you are reading this book, compared to my present time that I am writing this book. You and I only have our faulty perception of what is occurring within each of us and what others share about themselves. As of this writing, I do not have the ability to pop into your head, and you cannot pop into my head to do as you will.

But the Author of the Story we are in, like an author in his/her own story, has access to all characters and all things that can be known in all time frames, at the same time. I don't know about you, but I want some of that God revelation. Not for my own self-serving ways (hopefully!) but to further the Story of my Author, with the role I have. I am limited to a street-level view within the confines of my vision of the world, and God has an entire universe-and-beyond view, with no limitations of space, time, and energy.

Imagine running late for a difficult day of work filled with deadlines you are not sure you can meet. Now you are walking down the street with Jesus beside you. You turn your head in all directions. Strangers walk ahead and past you. Several homeless people are asleep beside you. A drug deal to your right. Someone walking toward you intentionally bumps into you as they pass by. Everyone is looking at their phone.

You panic when Jesus is no longer beside you. Then a strange peace moves within you. Now God gives you His POV while *within* you. You have Jesus's eyes. You have Jesus's thoughts. Your steps morph into His. You feel different. You feel lighter. More free. Things are now different around you. Most people around you have something else operating within them, and it is not Jesus. People don't know their Story, so they don't know their Author. They are bound in old ways and wounds, stuck, asleep, and without liberty of movement and strength.

Your chest burns within. You don't know anyone around you. But you do. And you love them. Each person.

Your Author, your God, is the only One fully capable of seeing within and through, and able to examine through every wall of every building and every heart. Including the one who is His living and moving temple.

He makes Himself known within you not only for His benefit but for yours. His love, His truth, His vision examines all parts of you, and all others, all at the same time, with flashbacks, flash-forwards, flash-sideways, past, present, future. He sees and communicates through all walls of all people and buildings, and He messages us and encourages us to move His hand while in conversational prayer.

Bottom line is that we have sin and spirit wounds from injuries we commit against ourselves, against others, and sins of others committed against each of us. We even have church wounds, as those in churches with their own wounds then injure us and vice versa. It comes down to sin. Every spirit wound that causes invisible scar tissue, that causes pain and limitations in strength and movement, eventually can be tracked down to a sin or sins committed. By me. By you. By others.

We each have a backstory of sin, wounds, injuries, and spiritual scar tissue. Only the Author knows the whole Story, not just parts of it but all parts big and small. He offers to guide you as you exercise spiritual muscles to walk away from the confines and limitations of your sins and scar tissue while hiding behind trees covering your nakedness. He invites you to walk toward Him and away from self-induced atrophy and fear.

If you have acknowledged and confessed your sins, believe Jesus died for your sins, and have committed yourself to and asked Him to enter your life and heart, this same God and Savior is within you. Living within you. From the temple in Eden, to the tabernacle traveling with the Israelites, to the temple in Jerusalem, to us being the temple, to us living in God. He is with us. He is within us. In the New Jerusalem we are within Him.

Oh, you and I still have pockets of resistance to Him that Satan attempts to expand as he colonizes parts of our hearts for his gain. But God will show you how to allow Him to expand within you. You can know Him, who unveils and frees you from your fear of death and rejection, laziness, addictions, and self-centeredness.

A Mere Glimpse into God's Very Nature

We have major hints about who God is with the first verse in the Bible. "In the beginning God created the heavens and the earth" (Gen. 1:1)

Look familiar?

Within that first sentence we explicitly have God, creator of all things, who is outside of time. Implicitly, what goes along with these qualities? He must be an incredible Creator with incredible abilities for precise and massive power, design, purpose, knowledge, and love for His creation.

Or in more theological terms, He is omnipotent (all powerful), omniscient (all knowing), omnipresent (everywhere), omnibenevolent (all loving).

We must submit our idea of self, student, story, and Savior to where it belongs.

In Him.

God is omnipotent. I am not

God is omniscient. I am not.

God is omnipresent. I am not.

God is omnibenevolent. I am not.

God is eternal and beyond the confines of time and space. I am not.

God created everything from nothing. I have created nothing from nothing.

God is God. I am not.

God unveils these biblical principles as we walk with Him. Jen Wilkin, in her book *None Like Him: 10 Ways God Is Different from Us*,[17] further personalizes and compares the qualities of God and us. It is an encouraging and full of hope and sobering read.

Accurate intel is valuable in love and war. God can empower me, as God is within me to navigate the minefields and difficulties in this war zone we live in, with love, joy, and faith from the love and intel of the One commander in chief. Only He is God, beyond the confines of time, and creator of all things, and far above the one who finds great wisdom in a bad dad joke. (Do you know why Spider-Man's evil twin failed his driving test? He was a bad parallel Parker.)

Let's look at our updated diagram 6.

All of the above reasons are why I want the Creator (Father God), the Savior God (Jesus), the Spirit (God the Holy Spirit), through the love and power of the Holy Spirit, navigating through me toward what is most important in life.

The Trinity. Love and relationship with God is what is most important.

It all points to Jesus.

Are there certain patterns He moves through in His Story within each of His believers that can guide us to what is most important in life?

---

[17] Jen Wilkin, *None Like Him: 10 Ways God Is Different from Us* (Crossway, 2016).

It Always Comes Back to Story

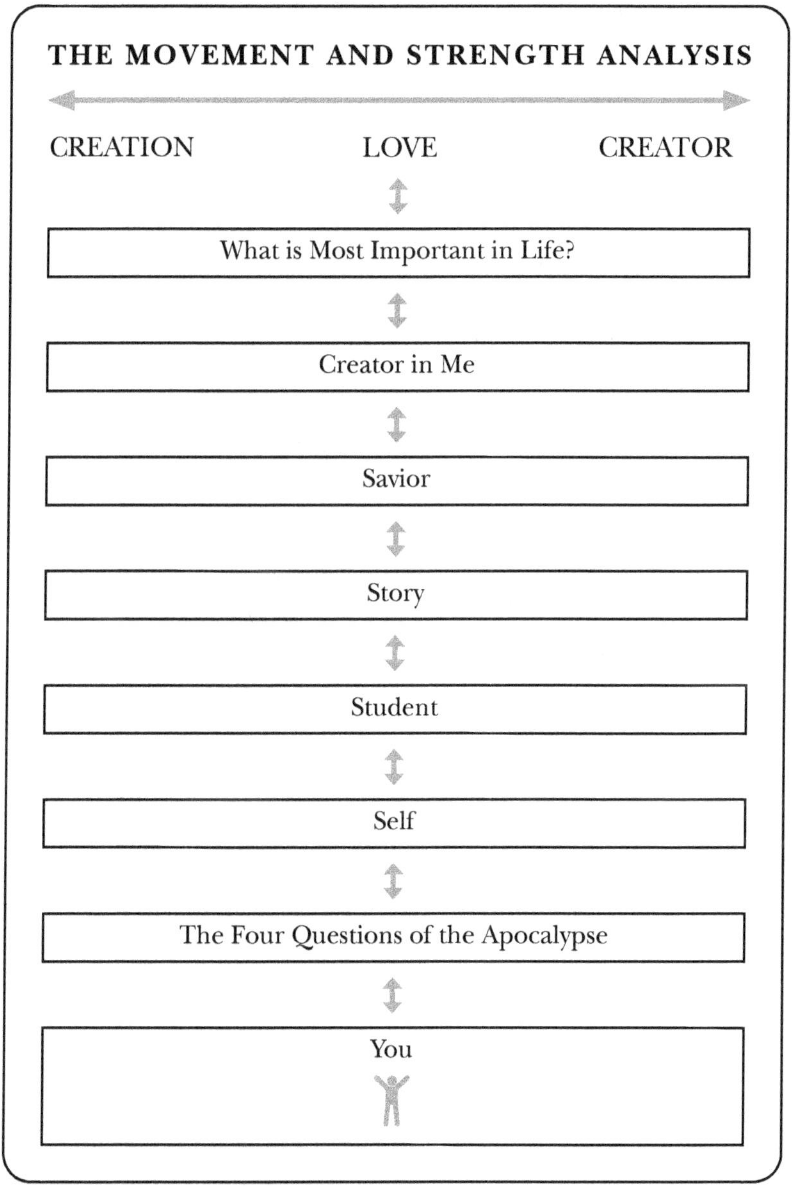

THE MOVEMENT AND STRENGTH ANALYSIS

CREATION   LOVE   CREATOR

What is Most Important in Life?

Creator in Me

Savior

Story

Student

Self

The Four Questions of the Apocalypse

You

Diagram 6

If there are certain patterns, I want to know them.
How about you?

Prayer

Lord,

You were with David when he suffered, and You hinted at Your own suffering through him. It makes sense to me that You can be with me as well. Be my Savior and live within me. Show me the hope I have in only You above all things.
Amen.

Questions

- When considering Psalm 22, can you name any other times in Scripture when God does some mind-bending things?
- Do you have a personal story about God doing something supernaturally, or an example involving someone you know?
- How would you describe the Savior and King of the world living within you?
- How would you feel, and live, if you found out that "God" was actually no different from you?
- How are you a really bad god?

CHAPTER 18

Your Great Physician's SOAP Note for You

In PT we document every patient visit and treatment with a SOAP note. What is a SOAP note, you ask? S stands for "subjective," O for "objective," A for "assessment," and P for "plan."

To discover the truth of their condition, I ask patients for clues. The subjective (S) part is what the patient tells me regarding how they feel and their sense about their condition. Is it a pain, numbness, tingling? They will also tell me when it started, where the symptoms are, and other qualities about their symptoms and the effects on their lives.

The objective (O) part is me documenting objective measurements and tests, like their range of motion, their strength, their neurological status, and responses to different positions and movement. Objective testing can also include x-rays and MRI results.

I then move to the assessment (A). Based on the subjective evidence combined with the objective evidence, I assess what I think is going on and make a plan (P) for what we are going to do.

It is my belief that we each do an internal SOAP note with most major decisions in life. Perhaps even all decisions. When trying to decide the truth of a situation, we use what we feel and sense as subjective evidence, combine that with objective evidence mostly separate from our subjective sense, make an assessment based on the subjective evidence and the objective evidence, and make a plan.

How does this work in the nonmedical realm? I am glad you asked. Let's say you are considering buying a car. You take it for a drive to see how it feels. Subjectively you feel it is a good drive. You like the looks. Lookin' good! And you love the warm memories that come with the car's smell.

Objectively, you want to know the cold, hard truth. You look at the cost, reliability, features, and gas usage and then objectively determine if you can afford it.

Based on your subjective feelings and sense about the car, and the objective factors, including the cost and your finances, you assess the full evidence and then make a plan to buy or not buy the car.

Let's say you are considering marrying someone. You think about how you feel about that person and your subjective senses of the overall situation. You consider the objective truth as to whether you should move forward. If the person is currently married or in prison for murdering their previous significant other, those objective facts might influence your decision. Based on what you feel and the objective facts, you make an assessment and then a plan to act accordingly. Marry or not marry.

God created us with a head *and* a heart. We are to think and feel. We are not to be like Spock, with few to no feelings, and we are not to be like SpongeBob SquarePants and cry and scream in emotion, above logic and reason, every episode.

God created us to move in both ways, in a subjective and objective sense mixed beautifully together. In essence we are to move in the Word and the Spirit. Wisdom would dictate that there is a subjective-feel aspect to living with Christ in us and the objective Word of God that transcends what we feel.

One of the more impactful stories in Scripture, for me, demonstrates how God uses the principles of a SOAP note. This makes sense because God created us with a head *and* a heart to navigate, even while submitted under the objective truth of His Word, communicated through a subjective sense within us. Head and heart.

Here is some homework. In your Bible read Luke 24:13–35. Finished? We see two disciples of Jesus walking to the village of Emmaus after Jesus had been killed. Many were in mourning for the death of hope for a Savior to save them from government oppression. Their hope was now dead. His body was missing. While the two were talking about the events of the day, who walks up to them? The One who was dead and missing is now walking with them. The Bible tells us that "their eyes were prevented from recognizing Him" (v. 16).

How crazy is that? They are talking about the murder of the Messiah, how His body was missing, and then the missing body was now talking and walking with them without them realizing it. The hope and the presence of our Savior walked with them! Oh, and by the way, it was entirely possible, and may I say probable, that the supposedly dead Messiah was actually preventing them from seeing Him right before their eyes.

Jesus more or less asks them, "What's up, bros? What are you both talking about?" They then stop and looked sad. Then one of them more or less says, "Are you clueless? Are you the only one in Jerusalem who does not know what happened?" To which Jesus replies, "What things?" With non-seeing eyes they then try to open Jesus's eyes by reviewing, with the alive Jesus, what had happened to dead Jesus before He was dead Jesus, as the once-dead-but-now-alive Jesus was walking with them. This was all the same Jesus they'd known previously. Hilarious!

Now God is one and He does not change, but in a sense there was once a dead Jesus and now there is an alive Jesus. Same God. Same Jesus. Alive Jesus then tells them how it was necessary for alive Jesus to suffer and die and gives them perhaps the most stunning Bible Story, the Story, and reviewed Moses, the prophets, and the things that were said about Himself. This book you are reading is encapsulated in this one scene, as we in life seek to move with strength as we walk with our Author as He tells us His and our Story, which only He can open our eyes to see.

When the two travelers arrive at their destination, Jesus then acts like He is actually intending to walk farther (gotta love Jesus's humor here), and they practically beg Him to come and stay with them.

When Jesus dines with them, He takes the bread, breaks it, and gives it to them. (Oh, the Bread of Life breaking bread really gave it to them, all right). Then their eyes are opened. I am sure Jesus timed the life-changing punch line perfectly, and then He disappeared! Poof! Gone! Wow!

Their lives could never be the same after that. This is the part I want to emphasize. They then said, "Were not our hearts burning within us . . . while He was explaining the Scriptures to us?" (v. 32).

There it is. The Word and the Spirit. The SOAP note and Story and our walk all working together. The S for the subjective evidence (their hearts were burning within them), the O for the objective evidence (the Word of God and Jesus was with them), then the A for assessment (they weighed the subjective and objective evidence and determined it was Jesus risen from the dead), and then the P for plan kicked in as they moved with the power of God to share the good news with others.

All this could only make sense by utilizing the principles of Story by combining flashbacks of Jesus previously ministering with them, to then see in the present, God now telling them He was alive and with them, which would propel them into their future plan to tell others about Jesus. There was no making sense for themselves of what happened if they had no knowledge of how to structure story in their heads and hearts, or if they did not know the Story.

Whether we are deciding on a car or a house or a significant other, or reading about it in almost every page in the Bible, or just about anything else, we use the SOAP note.

Navigating Life

Let us look at our updated diagram 7 with our SOAP note.

We navigate through challenging questions, self mode, student mode, Story mode, Savior mode, and Jesus our Creator within us, using SOAP notes, all in varying order, just as we utilize in healthcare. But this SOAP note is from the greatest of all physicians, desiring to heal us from our sins and the invisible scar tissue from our spirit injuries.

This is the Savior and Great Physician operating within us to move in newfound strength. With Him dwelling within us, wisdom dictates we should utilize a healthy mix of the head and heart He has made, to guide us in everyday decisions. As the Word of God should trump our subjective feelings, God still uses our head with our feelings. We should use both our heart and head, feelings and wisdom, in a holy mix.

So where are you?

It Always Comes Back to Story

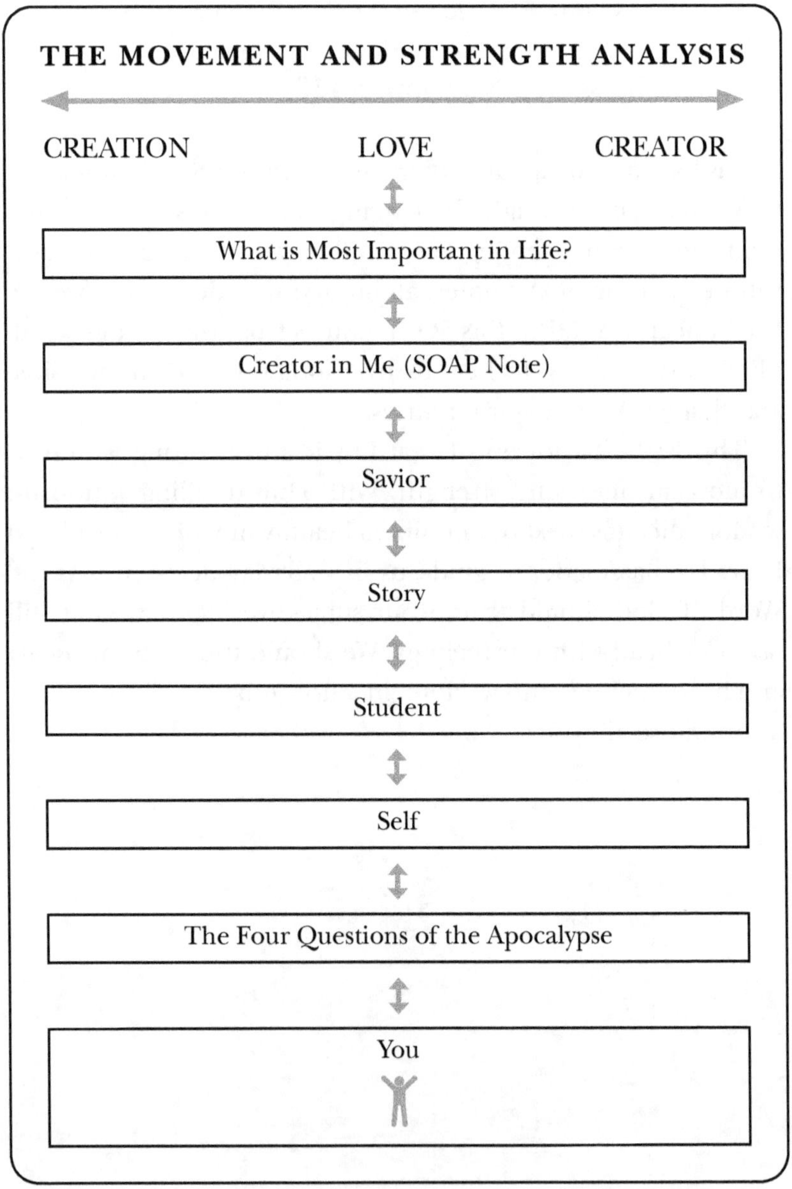

THE MOVEMENT AND STRENGTH ANALYSIS

CREATION   LOVE   CREATOR

What is Most Important in Life?

Creator in Me (SOAP Note)

Savior

Story

Student

Self

The Four Questions of the Apocalypse

You

Diagram 7

Prayer

Lord,

I want to navigate and flourish in this life with You within me. You have created me just the way You planned, so move through me in all the ways You have created me to do your will. Use my gifts, my strengths, my scars, and my head and heart. You created me. Shape me, mold me, into who You desire.

Have Your way in my life,

In Jesus's name.

Amen.

Questions

- Can you think of a time when God used your head and heart to teach you something?
- Why did God give you a head and heart?
- What would happen if you only used your head and not your heart?
- What would happen if you only used your heart and not your head?
- If God created you with a head and a heart to use in life, what does that tell you about your Creator?

CHAPTER 19

A Case Study for a Friend

God wants to heal and break through our spiritual scar tissue. You have probably been thinking of your own personal circumstances and wondering how all of this stuff works in a more tangible way.

In physical therapy literature, one can find case studies of specific patients highlighting certain treatments. Let's use a case study to see how you may move in an everyday life situation, based on what we have covered so far.

Let's suppose you desire to converse with someone you care about. Perhaps you want to share how your journey with this book has gone. Or maybe you have been a Christian for a long time and are looking for ideas on how to even start a conversation that would then eventually lead to further deep talks.

Let us explore in conversation how all this may look.

A Case Study

I want you to imagine growing closer to a friend, perhaps a coworker or neighbor, during a time when you both are having some challenges in your lives. Your friend is going through a season of reflection on life.

This life is difficult. It is easy to get distracted. But even in the midst of challenging times, let us not forget what is most important in life. Love and relationships. That includes love and relationship with how you view yourself, as well as with family, friends, acquaintances, and people you do not yet know well. And the love and relationship with God is preeminent and above all other loves and relationships.

God has softened your heart, which often defaults to self mode, and you count as a blessing the invested time and emotions of your relationship with this particular friend. Let's call him Lane (feel free to make your friend either male of female).

As you know, relationships are important in so many ways. First, you have someone you can connect with. Someone you can share the wounds and scars and joy with.

Also, if Lane is struggling, he knows you care for him. And vice versa. You have his best interest at heart, and he knows that. This is such an important foundational structure to build upon when discussing deep and weighty issues. Discussing, or attempting to discuss, deep and challenging topics without an already good relationship can actually hurt a relationship if it is not done in God's way and timing.

The times I could tell you when I have tried to force a discussion that was not in His timing and in His ways! But also there have been times where I knew He desired for me to confront some difficult truths for myself or others, and I did not. I honestly don't know which is worse, having the regret of forcing a conversation or having the regret of not pursuing a conversation.

But I do know that regret is one of the worst of all emotions. So I try to be ready for when the Lord calls on me. I find it helpful to be reading and studying the Bible and engaging in conversation with God at all times. Use the SOAP note to dialogue with God about His way and timing. That is always a great place to start.

Both you and Lane decide to go on another long walk in a scenic area. Walks always get the thinking and talking juices flowing.

You have been progressively moving out of a difficult season in your life. You have learned some great lessons as you have increased your times with God. You are growing.

Your heart is heavy for Lane's challenges. Lane is stuck in his invisible spiritual scar tissue. Pretty much immobile in a significant area in his life. You see it. You know it because every day you are gradually breaking through your own internal spiritual web. He sees it within himself with clarity at times, though other times it is not clear at all. You ask yourself, *What is the most important thing in life to him?* You suspect that question has not been answered in the way that would free him.

Take another look at diagram 7 from bottom to top.

Remember that the diagram is just a guide on how we usually move. It is not a step-by-step recipe to follow. Seek God and you may find that you only talk about the Story of Scripture (that is certainly powerful enough!) and how your friend may fit. Or you may cover one of the four questions. Or perhaps you end up talking about humility and testing one's beliefs by being a student of life. Or maybe talking about our self-centered tendencies or the need of a Savior. Let the Spirit guide.

Let's go.

"Lane, I always appreciate getting together with you. Thanks for joining me for another walk. I hope lunch is on our schedule afterward."

"Charlie, same here. And yes. Your idea is the carrot before me."

"I see what you did there. Food often unites us toward a common cause!"

"As you know, I am going through a tough time. I have never had an illness like this in my life before. I am running out of time to find that future wife of mine you have been praying for me to meet. Thank you for being there for me. I thank you for your friendship."

"It is an honor to pray for you. You have a good medical team helping you. I know you are looking for direction and asking good questions about life in general. We've been around the block a few times."

"I see what you did there . . . Something is off with me and in the world. Though the loneliness is still with me, I also can't figure out why I don't feel quite right, even beyond the medical diagnosis."

"I have learned something so simple yet so profound that it has transformed me and the way I view things. Can I share what I have learned with you? Maybe it will help?"

"Absolutely."

"It *always* comes back to Story."

"I can't wait to hear how you're going to explain that one."

"It helps me set the framework for everything. It helps connect dots with the important questions in life. Are you ready?"

"You know I love good questions. Challenge me."

"Several of my relatives in my story had some close calls and nearly died before I could be born. Serious car crashes, cancer, shot at, house fires. And as you know, I myself have had a handful of close calls. If any of my previous relatives in my immediate ancestral line would have died too soon, I would not be here right now. With my close calls alone, I could very easily not be here. I could tell you some stories. But yet I am alive."

"I hear you. I could say the same. Especially with what the doctors are telling me today."

"*Why are you alive?*"

At this point, the discussion can really take off. I am seeking God with the SOAP note in my head and heart, utilizing previous parts of our story together—consisting of the conversations and times I have spent with God and with Lane. It is an ongoing dialogue that I am becoming more well versed in. God uses it to help me navigate. I am in continual conversation with God on what *He* wants to do, using the subjective evidence of God communicating with me submitted under the principles of His objective Word.

I am continually asking God to help me assess the subjective and objective evidence of the present situation. The tone and momentum of the conversation will probably demonstrate all of the above and will also help guide. I then move on with His plan.

This first of the four questions may be the central focus of a fruitful first conversation. It may be all the entire conversation consists of. Or I may get a resounding stop to the conversation and then seek God for another opportunity at another time. Or maybe it is time to ask one of the other four questions.

You are a quarterback with some training and with some basic knowledge of the playbook, but when you are at the line of scrimmage in the conversation, He can call an audible. He may communicate a different play and tell you to go in a different direction. Follow what God is doing with you and your friend at that particular moment. It may not be the right time for the big questions.

Sometimes with these questions, stories explode into action, and sometimes more backstory and exposition is needed before that time can come. Backstory and exposition (exploring the subject matter in detail) is necessary to move into exploding action. Your friend probably has some stories of his own parents, grandparents, where they could have died before your friend was born. Your friend probably has had a close call or two in the past if he has lived long enough. Just follow the Author and let Him weave a Story before both of your eyes, at His pace.

You can't rush art!

In this case study, I will continue with the rest of the conversation to review the other questions and the rest of the diagram, but the timing of each question should be out of your control. The questions may occur in different order and pacing. They may happen in one conversation or be in parts of several future conversations. Again, follow the Author.

Imagine that your friend has paused to reflect on your question.

"Wow, Charlie. Why am I alive? I have not really considered that question before. I think I am alive to be happy."

"Okay, Lane. I am going to go ahead and ask a second question. As you know, I love to share time with God in nature. I love spending time with family and friends, like you. I love to write. I love to exercise. *What do you live for?*"

"I think if I am honest, I live to fulfill my hopes and dreams and to help others fulfill theirs. There might be more than that, but I would have to think about it."

"Thank you for sharing, Lane. I know you have helped me in many different ways, my friend. I have another question for you. When I think about it, I must make decisions all the time in which I have to do what I think is best under all sorts of circumstances. When all is said and done, when you have to choose what you will do on a moment-by-moment basis, *who do you live for?* Who ultimately drives you and your decisions?"

"Hmm. These are all deep and probing questions. I like this. I know I can trust you. I guess when all is said and done, I have to be the one to decide what is best regarding my own personal issues."

"That makes sense. Are you ready for what I have found to be the ultimate reality check?"

"You mean it gets deeper?"

"Buckle up your scuba gear. We're gonna go in deeper waters."

"I know the water is cold, but this won't be the first time. Let's jump in."

"Sometimes I imagine what it would be like in my last few moments, days, or weeks on my deathbed. I hope I will know what's truly valuable at that time. Will I be telling myself, 'I should have worked more hours at my job'? Or 'I wish I had more money right now. I wish I had a nicer home. A nicer car right now.' Or maybe 'I wish I would have argued more with my family. I should have destroyed all my relationships.'"

"You are funny. I don't think anyone has those regrets in life's final hours."

"I pray that if I have that day where my life is truly winding down, I will have finally gotten to the root core issue of life. The meaning of life. *What is most important in life?*"

I pray that you and I will not die hating ourselves, and/or alone, after years of toxic views of ourselves and others, along with resulting stupid decisions and the destruction of relationships with family and friends we once had. Even if that happens, if you are alive and aware enough, it is not too late with our relationship with God, and then perhaps with others. If we are still alive, still able, then we can seek God to make our relationship with Him right, and then with ourselves and others.

We can still choose where to place our ultimate love and allegiance. Let us now focus on what is most important in life while we are still alive! And if you are like me and have believed lies about yourself and others, said things that hurt relationships, then make things right and chase after what is most important while you still can. Your ego . . . my pride . . . is not what is most important in life. We can't have an accurate view of who we are, and others, until we live what is most important first. It is God. I pray that on our deathbed we would know who we are in God and be surrounded by those we love and who love us.

Living what is most important and sharing this with others is what this whole book is really about. If you think about it, that is what God's message to us—His Word, the Bible—is really all about. Moving in strength with love and relationships. This is Life 101.

Everything else is less important.

People sometimes answer all of these questions with "I don't know." This can be an honest answer. This can also be an attempt to not be forthright because of the possible consequences of honest answers.

Keep in mind, even if your friend is unsure or does not explicitly give answers, he still has answers. A nonanswer is still an answer. In reality, with our fallen human nature, we usually answer the four questions with "me."

The big, dirty secret is that if I am apart from God, I live for what will make *me* happy. I live to be happy and to meet *my* needs and desires above God. I live for myself, when all is said and done. My happiness and desires are what become most important in life. And our actions illustrate this. We may have flashes of unselfishness at times, but even our flashes of unselfishness are quite often an attempt to satisfy ourselves and our conscience, to try to lessen the guilt of not putting God above all.

Note diagram 7 again as we work our way up from the bottom to the top to what is most important. Hopefully the Four Questions of the Apocalypse has helped us to see the judgment upon the status quo mediocrity and to see beyond the self.

Self

"Lane, the questions I asked you are questions that I continue to ask myself almost every day. When I am honest with myself, past the superficial niceties, I learned that I answered the four questions with *me* as the answer to all four of the questions! I centered everything around me. I found it to be an empty life. I am a terrible god. I learned there is much more than myself. There is a beautiful life beyond and greater than myself."

This is a huge step to see beyond oneself. Is this not the root of all sin? Is this not the root of our spirit scars? At some point with each of my own sins and spirit injuries, I sinned, and/or someone sinned against me.

Student

"Bear with me, Lane. I also learned that the best way to get over myself was to adopt the attitude of a student of life. I do not know all things. Actually, I know few things when I compare myself to all that can be known. Every great student has to have *humility*. I don't have all the answers. I had to humble myself to learn truths beyond myself. It led me to God being my ultimate Teacher. And every great student has to be tested. How can I know that what I believe is accurate without testing my knowledge? How can I know that what I believe is reality and that I have not deceived myself? To live life untested is a weak, selfish, and untested faith in only myself. No wonder I struggled with fear, stress, and anxiety. I was living an untested life. I finally humbled myself at the feet of the Teacher, and I put all my beliefs to be tested by the Teacher. Now I live more confidently, as my beliefs have been well tested. Forged in the fire."

"I suppose that all that makes sense."

"And how do we make sense of what is important in life without humbling ourselves and testing our beliefs?"

"You and I know that our fallibilities, our flaws, our strengths, all play a role in how we view things. I guess in each of our own eyes, we just try and do our best."

Now might be a great time to move toward the next mode of truth. Again, the entire diagram may or may not go in sequential order for you. It may only consist of perhaps one of the questions, or none, or just humility. It may consist of prayer together.

It may not consist of any of the principles we've gone over. Often God desires us to rest and share in a good relationship.

For the sake of the principles we have covered, let us continue in the order of the diagram from the bottom toward the top.

Story

"Like I said before, it always comes back to Story. You and I love stories. How much do you invest in your entertainment, which consists of stories? Think of your favorite movies, books, TV programs, podcasts, songs, or artwork. When we get together, we first like to catch up on each other's stories. You and I have used, and presently use, stories to help us navigate and make sense of life."

"Perhaps we are communicating right now with story, Charlie."

"Exactly! You have over time created a story about me inside your head, and I have done the same about you. That is how you make sense of me and that is how I know you."

"That is how I sometimes think some of your ideas are crazy conspiracy ideas."

"Exactly! I have composed stories in my head that make sense to me and therefore are reasonable conspiracies. Reasonable . . ."

"Well, fallen angels and humans reproducing together . . ."

"Hey now . . . some of that is in my book, so don't distract our readers."

"Ha!"

"But you just helped me make my point. You had to construct a story about me to even make sense of what I am saying, and you need to have a story of me to make sense of disagreeing with me."

"A little crazy at times, but always interesting. I guess my computer knowledge can come into play here. I think you are saying that I have a Charlie Program and I have been entering data about you whenever we spend time together, and I am always evaluating the data to derive a conclusion on a moment-by-moment basis."

"That is good. I like that."

"But my assessment of the data is only as good as the data I enter. And I can input accurate data and then make a false assessment of that data. Accurate data. False assessment. Or inaccurate data and a false assessment of reality. I think I see where you are going."

"Now you know, Lane, better than anyone, that I am a techno weakling. But I know how to evaluate and write stories. Your data is backstory and exposition to me. And every great story has an author. The author usually uses a main point of view, along with other points of view, to tell the story, and the author edits the story to make it more effective. The same components of story that an author utilizes are the same components we use when composing our everyday and every-moment stories, which we narrate in our heads to help us make sense and navigate life."

"I think I see where you are going with this."

"Does it make sense that Frodo, a character, demands and tells Tolkien, the author, what to write? Does it make sense that an orc can adopt Frodo's point of view to understand everything that Frodo sees and knows? No, because that was not the author's intent in *The Lord of the Rings*."

"The author ultimately determines what his story is. Not a character in the story. And the author decides which POV, and through which character, he tells the story."

"Right once again. What if real life is that way as well. Here is the plot twist in our discussion. We love good stories that we can escape into, when in reality we *live* in a bigger Story than our own. God is the Author and He is the main point of view, though He allows us freedom to make choices through our individual points of view. He knows all the different information, He creates the data, and only He knows all the points of view of everyone and everything in the Story at any time. We do not have all the information, or all the data, or all points of view because we are not God, the Author, and it is His Story, not yours. And certainly not mine. I sin when I attempt to hijack His Story and attempt to make it my own above His."

"I think I understand what you are saying, Charlie. That means He is the writer *and* editor of the Story. He ultimately decides what goes into the Story and what does not. Just as you can't edit my own story in my head, and I cannot yours, so it is that we cannot rewrite and edit what the main Author has in His Story, which is bigger than us."

"You are seeing better than me. Preach it, brother."

"Perhaps we get into trouble when we take convenient parts of the Author's Story and try to remake it into our own story."

"That is plagiarism. When we take what is His and make it our own, with no acknowledgment that it was from Him."

"Ow. That one stung."

"I am stinging right now just bringing it up. We cannot hijack God's Story and make it our story, and ourselves the author, main point of view above all others, and editor, because that was not the Author's intent. It always comes back to Story. It always comes back to the Author of the Story. So now, why are you alive? What do you live for? Who do you live for? What is most important in life?"

"This is all really stretching me . . . but ultimately this is really good. And also strangely comforting. Full of ultimate hope that is greater than me and takes pressure off of me. This is freeing. Because I can't do this on my own. I need help. I have some things to think about."

"Genesis one verse one. Interestingly, the first sentence in God's Story tells us some significant things. The first sentence says 'In the beginning God created the heavens and earth.' Just the wording of that first sentence tells us we are going to experience quite the epic tale. But this narrative is true. This is our first hint that we are in a Story, and every story has different points of view, and right there with the first sentence, we have at least two points of view in the Story. Do you see it?"

"I never thought about it before. I have read that very sentence and heard it many times. But there it is in plain sight. Creator. Creation."

"You are good, Lane. Two possible points of view. In that first sentence, there is also a foreshadowing of the coming conflict. There is also a hint of the resolution of the conflict. I could spend the next hour talking about all the other things packed into that first sentence, but for now let's just focus on one main theme. How do we view the Story we live in? Through the Creator's eyes or through the eyes of creation? We live in the tension between these two points of view. That is our Story."

"Charlie, what chance do we have when ninety-nine percent of all stories we consume, stories we see with books, movies, TV, are told from a perspective that is not from the Creator? What chance do we have of making sense of the Story we are in when ninety-nine out of one hundred times the stories we take in and compose in our heads are not from God's point of view. We have no chance."

"I think God has given us ways to see where we are going, because God will hold us accountable. Think of a Movement and Strength Analysis, where there are the two points of view on opposite sides of a line. Creator. Creation. Where are each of us trending as we place our ultimate love and allegiance? Where are we getting our movement and strength, our power from? God heals us of our spirit wounds, in a sense, breaking through our spirit scar tissue, as we gain liberty of movement and strength when we move toward the Creator. We get stuck, locked in loss of healthy movement and strength from our spirit injuries and invisible scar tissue, when we gravitate toward, and give our ultimate love and allegiance, to creation."

"We have no chance. Our history demonstrates more slavery than liberty."

Savior

"I agree. We have no chance. And yet we are still responsible for our choices. But what if God is not only our Author and main point of view but is also the protagonist, our hero. Our Savior. You can search and research and compare all you want for the best savior, but I will tell you that Jesus will be the best Savior you will ever find."

"Charlie, you sound like my grandma on her deathbed years ago."

"What did she tell you?"

"She said, 'Boy, get your Story straight. It is Jesus.'"

"Ha! She said in one simple sentence what I am struggling to communicate in a book-amount of information!"

"I think I might want to read that book!"

"Maybe someday I will sit down and write that book and share it with you."

"You are funny."

"But you are right. Without a Savior, we have no chance. We can't do it. But He can. He already did. And because He did, we can see the truth of Satan's lies and move today with the Savior within our body, soul, and spirit to navigate this life."

"This is intense. But it seems right. Feels right."

"Lane, I am limited with all my spirit injuries and wounds caused by my sins and the sins of others. My invisible spiritual scar tissue limits all I should be. But God has healed me and is healing me. I acknowledged before God that He is God, not me. I confessed my many sins and asked for His forgiveness. I believed that He died for my sins, asked Him into my heart, and I committed my life for Him. Only with the Savior within us can we then move toward what is most important in life. Love and relationship with God first, which then forms the foundation of all other relationships. Now I can answer those four questions with new life. Now I know my 'why' in life is Him. He is what I live for. He is who I live for. He is most important in all of life. My Savior saved me from myself. This is my Story. This is your Story."

"This makes sense."

The Savior Living in Me, and the SOAP Note

"I have sometimes been stuck in convenient self mode and made myself the author, main POV, and editor of inconvenient parts, and have plagiarized convenient parts of His ways and tried to make them my own. I finally admitted that He was my Author, and I asked for forgiveness of my sins for all the times I tried to hijack what is His. And I asked Him to enter within me as my Savior and main POV."

"That is what changed you?"

"That is what transformed me. I am brand new. And now today I live and navigate life with Him within me. There is a *subjective* sense of learning to hear His voice, along with an *objective* truth—His Word, His Bible—that guides me beyond my subjective whims and biases. I then ask Him to help me make an *assessment* of the subjective and objective evidence, and then He gives me a *plan* to walk in that."

"Charlie, this sounds like you are loving, being loved, conversing, and living with a significant other above all others. You are newly married, in some sense."

"Great insight. So we come back full circle. It always comes back to Story. What is most important in the Story? Love and relationships. Within ourselves, with others, and with God above all. The great Story always points back to the Author. Can I tell you more about the only one, true Author, who heals us—yes, He heals us, transforms us, and restores us? Can I tell you about the One who shows me how to recalibrate, the One who sets my compass, my GPS, toward what is most important in life? Can we pray together that you would see that Jesus has been with you the whole time? Let's pray to see that He is the Author of your faith, that your ultimate marriage is that you can be part of the bride, and He is the groom, and that the Author and Creator will heal you."

Let's unpack what just happened.

Prayer

Lord,

I believe in You. I believe in Your Word. I confess I have tried to hijack Your Story when it was convenient and when I selfishly tried to change it into my own. Forgive me for when I thought I was the Author, I was the main protagonist, I was the editor, and when I plagiarized Your principles.

I turn away from my old ways.

I desire to follow the voice of my Shepherd.

Lead me.

Amen.

Questions

- How are you answering the Four Questions of the Apocalypse these days?
- When do you choose self over Savior?
- How does God's Story fit in the case study with Lane?
- Is it possible to navigate toward what is most important without a Savior?
- What would happen to your emotional life, your mental health, if you consistently recalibrated and sought out what was most important in life?

CHAPTER 20

Connecting the Dots and Pixels

In the last chapter, I presented some general principles in a possible everyday discussion. Again, you may only focus on one, or some, of the four questions. I find it most helpful to reorient back to what is most important in life, along with the other questions, and then go from there. What else deserves more attention than that which is most important?

I can personalize things by giving my own personal story with examples in the parts of the diagram I choose. Going from bottom to top on the diagram, I could talk about the emptiness and dead end when centering on myself. I can talk about being a student in life in humility and with testing. I can share what it looks like to live in the wrong story and how I cannot navigate this life well without my Savior within me.

I can share how I use the SOAP note by utilizing my God-given subjective sense of God communicating with me, while comparing and submitting to His objective Word, to assess and then move with a plan that will make Him smile.

Overview So Far

We have come a long way. Let's summarize where we are. We started with a woman burning down a house to cover up the crime of abducting an infant from her mother and her home. The kidnapper raised the child for about six years, with a different identity, a different mother, and a different home and life.

But the little girl's true mother never gave up the possibility that somehow her daughter was somewhere still alive.

God has not given up on you, and He still calls you back home with Him.

Let's take another look at our updated diagram 7.

It always comes back to Story. What kind of story have you believed about yourself? Where are you? Where have you placed your love? Who gave you your identity? In whose strength and power do you move in?

Reading Scripture, I believe you can find examples of spirit scar tissue, memories of past hurts and wounds, impeding movement and relationship with God in just about every person. How about Adam and Eve hiding after they sinned? How about Abraham lying to protect himself on at least two different occasions? Moses telling God that he, Moses, was not a good speaker? Sarah laughing before God about getting pregnant? Elijah and Jonah running in fear from God's will? Peter losing focus and falling into the sea and later denying Jesus? Paul persecuting Christ followers before his conversion? There are many more examples of a wound to a person's immaterial part, their emotional health, their soul and/or spirit, and a corresponding fear that then limits that person's movement and power in relationship with God.

It affects their faith.

It affects our faith in God and who He is and who we are. With our wounds, we then operate out of the flesh and not the Spirit.

Is it not interesting that we can see evidence of sin, and spirit scar tissue, and the corresponding limitation of strength and movement in just about everyone in Scripture except Jesus, and yet it is by Jesus's wounds and scars that *we* can be free from *our* sin and can have *His* strength and power within *us*?

It Always Comes Back to Story

THE MOVEMENT AND STRENGTH ANALYSIS

CREATION   LOVE   CREATOR

What is Most Important in Life?

Creator in Me (SOAP Note)

Savior

Story

Student

Self

The Four Questions of the Apocalypse

You

Diagram 7

Wounds and ensuing spirit scar tissue can open us up to Satan and his proxies influencing us and wreaking havoc within our heart homes (more on this later in this book series).

As we move in this world, there are many competing affections. There are the distractions of what our culture tells us are most important, that pull and tug at us, and we end up moving in the wrong direction, trying to self-medicate our injuries and traumas, attempting to find freedom and strength of movement.

But we get stuck. Locked into our limited ways. Often in the physical realm, moving impaired tissue causes more pain and can incentivize us to not move the painful part. Sometimes in the spiritual realm, moving our spiritual scar tissue and wounds also causes more pain and also incentivizes us to then immobilize. It is easy to decide to not move or to not move in such a way as to reproduce our pain. Our adversary abducts us and renames us away from who and where we should be.

Satan's false name and identity for us is based upon a lie. We can become isolated and disconnected from God. We gradually drift and walk away from God and get stuck in a status quo of mediocrity in our spiritual landscape.

It always comes back to Story, and Genesis 1:1 is a great place to start the Story. Perhaps it is time to release the Four Questions of the Apocalypse to judge our status quo mediocrity.

Why am I alive?

What do I live for?

Who do I live for?

What is *most important* in life?

Standing with an adversary and his proxies, who are stronger than any human power we possess, we raise our hands up in surrender.

What a wonderful place to be! Just like when someone struggling with an injury finally decides to get help from those with greater skills and knowledge in physical rehabilitation than themselves, how marvelous it is when someone struggling with invisible injuries and scar tissue from sin finally decides to seek help, even salvation, from the Great Physician. He teaches us that in Him we have greater power, skills, and knowledge than our enemies will ever have. Wounded, broken, perhaps spiritually dead, and falling into the pit of their own strength and movement, now seeking help!

God evaluates our walk with Him or away from Him. The Great Physician has His own movement and strength analysis, which gives us an idea of how we are walking.

Where are you?

What is most important in your life?

The four questions prime us to now take a closer look. Are you moving away or toward God? We concluded that the most important thing in all of life is love and relationships and the most important love and relationship is our love and relationship with God.

Recalibrate

Here is a great calibrating question: Are you moving toward or away from what is most important in life?

Recalibrate. How do we move toward God in love and relationship? Did the four questions expose why I am stuck, impaired in my movement and strength? Have I placed myself above God? Did I answer the four questions with me above God?

In our spiritual walk and journey, we can move through different stages and phases in our lives, through truth modes from self mode, student mode, through Story mode, with our Savior, who moves within us toward what is most important in life.

How many of us are stuck in various degrees of the self mode?

Are we actively engaging at all times in the student mode by living with humility and testing all our beliefs and ideas, using God and His Word to better understand His thoughts?

Are we living toward what is most important in life, or are we distracted with something or someone else attempting to replace what is most important in life?

We can't do this in our own power. We sin and fall for Satan's trap virtually every moment in life. We need a Savior. Creation is not our Savior.

The Four Questions of the Apocalypse expose us and who we are. From this foundation you can learn that He has desires of His heart that He has implanted into your heart. This is what you live for. You live for Him. You are to move in His liberty and His strength to flourish in His love and relationship first, which then forms the foundation and framework for *all* your other relationships.

Using a SOAP note with God moving freely within us through the Word and the Spirit, we can see how we fit in life with God, others, work, money, sex, and so forth. Remembering Adam and Eve in the garden, let's get it right this time as we walk with Him.

Prayer

Lord,

Forgive me of my sins. I repent and turn away from those old sins. Heal me completely from all the effects of my sins and the sins of others. Free me from my old, invisible scar tissue from my spirit injuries. May I move in Your full liberty and strength and power. Show me how to learn and live in the right Story with my only rightful Author. You have given me freedom to make choices throughout my life, and I choose You. You are my Story. You are my Author. Show me our Story, and show me my place in this world.

Amen.

Questions

- Have you ever felt like you were living in the wrong story?
- Have you ever felt like you were doing and living exactly the way you were created?
- What do you think it means to recalibrate and seek out what is most important in life?
- You have had your spirit injuries. You have had your spirit scars. How does your life look fully healed?
- Do you know others who have had their spirit injuries, scars, and scar tissue limiting their movement and strength?

CHAPTER 21

You Are New, for the Old Has Passed Away

It always comes back to Story. Your Author proclaims you are not who you think you are. Your story is not what you think it is. You are different than your former beliefs if you have given your life to the Author of your faith. You may think that who you are is based on your own POV and others' POV of you, but your Father, the Author and Creator of you, rescued you to tell you that in the only one and true authentic POV and Story, you are His.

You were made in the image of God. You are your Father's kid. You have the image of God—in essence, the Creator's spiritual DNA flows through you. Satan can try to take you away and lie and convince you that you are someone else, but you are God's.

Reading this book has hopefully given you some new insights and valuable life-changing intel. The four questions, the diagram, and the SOAP note (all shown at the end of this book), give you a better idea of how you fit in the greater big-screen picture and how to navigate toward what is most important.

Now you can see how others fit, how your loved ones see themselves and how they fit, in the Epic.

Our Movies

Could God have given us insights on who He is through Hollywood stories? Through an industry that is more often anti-God than honoring God?

Though there are some pearls in the large dumpster, five movies come to mind. Do you remember *Aliens? Seabiscuit? The*

Lord of the Rings? Saving Private Ryan? How about *The Map of Tiny Perfect Things?*

Satan and his proxies attach and attack us with tentacles spewing acid around and through us. This world grooms and trains us to lose. In our battle against foes much larger than us, will we risk everything to destroy the evil in our lives, to save others? Will we live and die for others above ourselves in this war? Will we discover that we have been living the wrong main POV all along and get our Story straight?

But when the Hero, the One who suffered for us, indwells in us, He re-creates us into new creatures with His transformational liberty training. The Author of the Story trains us to eventually destroy the plots and effects of our adversary, our antagonist, by taking on the hero's POV to save others.

Sacrificial Love

Think of the number of times people have given of themselves, and even their lives, to save yours. How many soldiers died in all the various wars of your country? How many relatives freely gave of themselves to preserve and save your relatives and ultimately you? Did your parent(s) freely give of their own lives for you to live?

How will you live your life knowing your Savior gave everything for you?

Evil, through sin, has inflicted many wounds and injuries, and the ensuing scar tissue once plagued you with loss of movement and strength in your walk and journey. But you know vital parts of the Story. You know you have a role.

In all the movies I mentioned, the viewer is invited to take on different POVs to get a fuller picture of the overall story. In my story, I was living life and navigating through all my weaknesses when my cousin was killed in the Vietnam War. He believed in freedom and traveled to the other side of the world to fight against those who opposed the values of liberty. He gave his life in this fight. The fear of death, with its alien tentacles, entered into me and attempted to take over my life. I feared death, and all the gradations and shadows of it, in the ensuing years. I had death's variations take hold of me with every health issue, a potential draft into the military, and it hovered over me, reminding me that I too would die in a foreign war.

But God used my cousin's story to free me of the stranglehold of the internal dictator, the scar tissue of death, to help free me of the despot and to help others as well.

The Old Dead Story

A story behind the song "Come, Thou Fount of Every Blessing" moves me almost as much as the song moves my heart and emotions every time I hear it or sing it. It's unverified, but it's widely told.[18]

I have wonderful memories of hearing this hymn every summer when our family was at family camp in the Santa Cruz mountains. A truly gorgeous area, if you ever have a chance to see the redwoods in the Santa Cruz, California, region.

But I think the song hits me even deeper than the wonderful family memories I have at family camp. There is a deeper hidden truth that hits me in ways I cannot explain. The song was written by Robert Robinson in 1758.

It is a beautiful melody with some beautiful lyrics. But part of the song is particularly haunting. If you know the song, you probably already know what part I am alluding to.

---

[18] The story can be found in multiple places online, including enjoyingthejourney.org, https://enjoyingthejourney.org/hymn-history-come-thou-fount/.

He wrote "Prone to wander, Lord, I feel it, prone to leave the God I love." The story goes that Robinson wrote these words in the zeal of his new life, with his Savior who saved him from gangs and alcohol and crime. He became a pastor and lecturer.

But he did wander. He drifted far from the God he loved. Years later on a ride, a young woman in the coach with him hummed a song. She asked him what he thought of the song "Come, Thou Fount of Every Blessing."

He more or less told her that in his current sorry state, he wished he could go back to those better days when he wrote that same song.

She then quoted his very words from the song and said, "Sir, 'the streams of mercy' are still flowing."

I remember years ago seeing a documentary where a woman who had years of heart problems had a heart transplant surgery. After the surgery, the nurses asked if she wanted to see her old heart. They took her to a room, and she stopped just short of the tray holding her once failing heart, and probably full of old scar tissue from all the previous heart injuries. She took and held her previous heart, and she wept.

Angela Davis had an amazing afro when she was younger. What amazing hair. She committed her life to the Black Panthers decades ago and fought against American capitalism and for black power and Marxism. She was, and still is, a prominent Marxist activist fighting against racism for decades.

Not too long ago she was on the TV program *Finding Your Roots*. What a great concept for a show. Several celebrities have gone on the program and had their ancestral lineage revealed for all the world to see. They did some testing and researching and revealed on TV that part of her ancestral lineage helped form the United States even before its birth upon the *Mayflower*. That would likely mean that some of her bloodline ancestors believed in capitalism, had slaves, and had ties to all the things she has fought against for most of her life.[19]

I remember decades ago when a pastor told a story that happened early in his ministry.

First a little background info. As you may already know, in some Christian circles a "word of knowledge" is when God reveals a specific truth that cannot have been known naturally. For example, you may be praying for someone and the Lord then plants a thought, a revelation, into your mind, and then you share this with the one you are praying for, and sure enough, it was a truth that only that person and God could have known. Truly a faith-building experience for all involved.

The pastor said that when he was starting a new church, he got a frantic phone call one evening from a leader of one of his Bible studies, asking the pastor to come to their group meeting. It was urgent.

The pastor arrived to find a member of the Bible study on one side of the room, breathing heavily, thrown furniture all around, and she was slithering and uttering deep guttural words. The other members stood shell shocked on the opposite side of the room, wide eyed.

One member told him that the petite female on the other side started throwing people and furniture and spoke with a voice that was not her own.

The pastor then rehearsed in his mind what to do if confronted with someone who was demon possessed. As he spoke to the young woman, the voice inhabiting her publicly exposed the pastor by announcing his private and personal sins for all

---

[19] "Angela Davis 'Can't Believe' Ancestry Revelations Going Back to the 1600s," *Today*, https://www.today.com/popculture/tv/angela-davis-finding-your-roots-mayflower -ancestors-rcna71700.

who were there to hear. Personal, private failures now in public before those who held him as their pastoral authority. He was fully exposed, with no tree to hide behind.

As he relayed the story, the pastor said it was a "reverse word of knowledge" in half-joking fashion.

The pastor was shaken, embarrassed, and prayed for help. A wave of God's strength moved through him, and he took hold of what was true. He boldly and confidently proclaimed directly to whatever was in the woman that that was his previous life. His old hijacked identity and name. He was now a new person. The old was dead. He proclaimed that he was forgiven of those past sins and was a new creature made by God. With the demon now weakened, the pastor then spoke to the lying spirit in the young woman, and God freed her from what colonized her.

I have wandered from God. I have had, and still have, my times of distraction, but today I seek Him above all. The old self is who I used to be. I can now look back at my old heart and thank my Savior that He now occupies a new heart, one that He remade in my chest. Every beat and missed beat of my heart is His. I am new. I am different than who I used to be.

I too have a history of previous ancestors who did horrible things in their past. I probably have a list of previous ancestors who were slave owners, racists, greedy capitalists, greedy communists, and other sins galore.

But you are new if you are in Jesus. The old has passed away, and you are a new creature. And He holds and lives in your new heart.

The little girl abducted in the beginning of our story was told that a liar and thief and child abductor was her mother. For six years this was the little girl's story.

Your life Story did not start with the sins of your ancestors. Though you have wandered, He has always been with you. Thank God for His grace extended to us, as whenever we complain about any people group and/or their beliefs, you and I have those same flaws we complain about running in our own blood. And you are not defined by a demon speaking to you or speaking about you.

You are new if you are in Jesus.

You have a new Story.

Prayer

Seek God and ask Him about your Story.

Lord,
Tell me who I am.
Amen.

Questions

- Can you name any movies or stories that can illustrate parts of your own personal story?
- What movie has spoken to you the most about who God is?
- Has someone given their life for you?
- Could you be where you are today without others sacrificing themselves?
- Is there someone you would freely give your life for?

CHAPTER 22

This Is Who You Are

It is worth remembering the concept of the unreliable narrator. It occurs when you are following a story through a narrator, and you wonder whether you can trust that narrator and their narration.

Using an unreliable narrator can be great for storytelling but is troubling when encountered in real life. It is difficult to fully trust a person who is not trustworthy in their storytelling.

Not only are we severely limited to just our narrow point of view, but on top of that, you and I are unreliable narrators in the telling of our individual stories. Challenges with our memory and the selective editing of not only our individual story but, even more so, when composing other peoples' stories are eye opening.

You and I have sinners in our lineage who rejected God with horrific consequences. And there is nothing you can do to undo those past effects. Do you remember the heartbreaking question God asked after Adam and Eve sinned and believed Satan in the garden?

"Where are you?"

If that was the first important question recorded in Scripture, later Jesus would ask his disciples perhaps the most preeminent question.

In Matthew 16 we read about Jesus asking His disciples who people said He was. They answered with the names of possible prophets. And then Jesus dropped the bomb with the important question.

"But who do *you* say that I am?" (v. 15, emphasis mine).

Simon Peter then said Jesus was the Christ, the Son of the living God. Jesus then told Simon Peter that he did not come to that truth from flesh and blood but by God revealing to him the truth (v. 17).

Look at the different POVs here in this smaller story and how they can fit in the bigger Story. First, Jesus asks what other people's POVs were of Him. There were many POVs. Then Jesus narrows the search and switches the POV to that of an individual disciple. Then Simon Peter uses his own POV to reveal the truth of Jesus's identity. Then Jesus assumes the ultimate POV and tells Peter how God the Father revealed His truth through His POV, through Peter.

Without God we are unreliable narrators assuming convenient selfish POVs, and we cannot find ultimate truth relying solely on our own power and POV. Only God through His POV can reveal that. We need to get our Story, Author, main POV, Protagonist, and antagonist straight.

You Could Not Be Stopped

But God is the most reliable of all narrators. And He is telling you that if He is within you as Lord and King, you are not who you think you are today. Your Story is not what you think it is.

Your life has not been wasted. You are not a loser. You are not a failure.

As a Christian, Jesus, the greatest life lived, is still living and is in your family line and flows within you and into others.

In Jesus you have a different Story. That is our Story. No matter how young or old you are today, your life Story is thousands of years old. Your real Story counters all threats, fears, lies, and time, as it predates you by thousands of years. It started with your Author already preexisting before time and creation itself.

Your adversary has attempted to stop your ancestors, to stop the seed from coming, and when he failed with that, he still today is attempting to stop the seed from returning. Along the way he is trying to also stop as many as possible from learning their true Story and their true Author and becoming followers of Jesus.

Satan's rebellion and influence of Adam and Eve's fall broke our DNA. But you have the spiritual DNA of God, and His Story, within you. Spiritual DNA of obedience and faith against death, and against the fears and judgment of others, are demonstrated in your spiritual ancestor Noah, who helped preserve the human race against the genocide attempts of Satan. Your spiritual ancestor helped save the human race.

You have within you the faithfulness and courage of Abraham to leave what was familiar and comfortable, to start a new nation and people to preserve humanity in a new home land. You have the DNA of Moses within you, who despite his difficulty in communicating, proclaimed freedom in the face of the power of Pharaoh. You have the spiritual lineage of the tenacity of Deborah to execute God's justice and to rule for a people moved toward God. You have the ancestral spiritual genes with the faithfulness and hope of Ruth gleaning with God. David the giant slayer and king. You have the DNA of Isaiah, who saw and lived the experience of the throne room of the living God. You have flowing in your veins the courage and wisdom of Daniel, who communicated God's proclamation of your future, which you are living in today. The spiritual DNA of the courage of Esther to risk her life to stop genocide runs in your blood.

You have the King of all kings, the One who served until death, the Author and Protagonist, Jesus, within you. You have in your spiritual family tree the desires of the first disciples to tell the Story, even under the threat of death.

You have the spiritual DNA of the same God who flowed through Paul, who moved from persecuting Jesus followers, to losing his eyesight, to then seeing God, to then becoming a spiritual giant through imprisonment and beatings, until death.

Do you think you lack direction, purpose, and conviction in life? Perhaps. But do not forget you have the spiritual DNA of Polycarp, who refused to renounce God while stabbed and burned at the stake. Your spiritual family includes John Wycliffe and William Tyndall, who lived through times of persecution and died believing that all people, not just the church, should be free to read God's Story without church powers dictating what you should and should not believe. You have the spiritual DNA of the courage of Dietrich Bonhoeffer, who communicated God's words under the reign of Hitler's Third Reich in Germany. Jim Elliot, and other missionaries and their wives, who refused to let the fear of death stop their missionary zeal. The power of the Coptic 21, who acknowledged God with a blade at their necks when they could have denied God and lived.

You also have the same spiritual DNA of the church and those who walk with God and who have strength to live out their Story underground in communist and Islamic nations, whose spilled blood does not stop the Story but actually fertilizes the soil for new growth.

You know you are not of this world's story. You know someone in your past spoke a lie and gave you a false identity. You are Spirit and flesh of another Story. The Author of the other Story speaks to you, gives you inklings about your spiritual heritage. He gives you revelation to help others stuck in the loss of liberty and movement and strength because they are in the wrong story, to move into their right Story.

I sometimes imagine our sins and spirit scar tissue are similar to invading weblike strands of unbreakable chains embedding into our strands of DNA. But when the Author of liberty enters into you, the strands of unbreakable chains embedded within your DNA break and become strands of multicolored unbreakable bands of lights of liberty, pulsating and ready to flow and move through your *new* DNA.

What beautiful lights your old scars and scar tissue are! Just as one of my patients, through exercise, pushes against scar tissue in a healthy way to improve movement and strength, so it is that God empowers you to stretch out of your comfort zone, sometimes in temporary discomfort, to then move in more liberty and strength and power than you had before the spirit injury. As a patient moves to finally believing that they can regain normal range of motion from an injured joint, so God can heal you and move you out of stiff and stuck relationships into new liberty.

God uses your injuries and wounds and breaks through old scar tissue to bring you to walk with your Author, freed up and strengthened. Does anyone ever come to God and acknowledge that He is the Author and main POV in all of life *without* pain caused by sin and evil? Is it possible to be convicted of our sins by the Holy Spirit *without* pain?

You will die one day (unless you are raptured first?!), but the King flowing within you will not be stopped and will resurrect you. Your Story is not one of failure but ultimate victory. Your scars of this life are evidence of Satan trying to stop you, but your adversary does not define you, for the Author, your Savior, has been with you the entire time—as He was with those possessing your spiritual DNA before you. You rightfully should not even be alive to read this book, but God has preserved those before you, and you are to be part of the remnant that speaks the power of the Story, that points to the Author, speaking truth in the face of lower-power authorities.

You have a great Story.

You have a great and wonderful Author.

You live in the Epic of all epics. You now know the vision and some of the scope of what God has done before you and for you. This Story then gives you the vision of hope and faith for the future, with full confidence, for if the Author was with those previous spiritual family members throughout Scripture, He is with you today for what lies ahead. Even in these difficult days. Even for the more difficult days coming.

Before you gave your life to Jesus, you were living in the wrong story. Like Frodo of *The Lord of the Rings* lost and wandering in *The Matrix,* how could you truly know who you are when you are lost in the wrong story?

A hard truth be told: Before you gave your life to Jesus, you were not fully connected to the most true, authentic, historical, genuine, and eternally transformative Story. You had lies of who you were. You had legends. You had myths of who you and your ancestors were, without true connection. You did not know how you were connected to your previous ancestors and their lives.

But that is no longer.

Several years ago I sensed the Lord revealing some interesting thoughts on the cross. Imagine a large horizontal beam representing the perfect holiness of God hovering over the earth. So holy that it could not touch creation, soiled with sin, without destroying creation. Now imagine a large vertical beam coming from heaven and piercing through the horizontal beam and claiming victory by striking His claim on the polluted and corrupted ground. The ground then becomes holy.

Not only does Jesus hold all things together (Col. 1:17), but on the cross He literally connected and bridged the holiness of the God of heaven to sinful earth, through His Godhood and through His humanity, through His holiness and through the sin He took on, and claimed victory by piercing and staking a claim over His turf. God and humanity, holiness and sin, life and death literally intersected with Jesus on the cross, who holds all things together. Jesus connected and bridged the holiness of the Creator in heaven with sinful creation on earth.

You are not alone, with only your adversary. From the first sentence in your Epic, He foreshadowed your victory. It is right there in Genesis 1:1. The Creator is the Protagonist, creation is the antagonist, the inciting incident is a clash between the Protagonist and His creation, the climax is the final battle between the Creator and creation, and the resolution is when the Creator becomes creation, though still God, to connect and bridge the divide between Creator and creation. He pierced the holy to strike a claim for what was not holy to become holy.

And He is within you, His mobile temple. You are dangerous and a threat to your adversary, as you are equipped with God's power and strength to resist and ultimately overcome Satan and his proxies. No more spiritual atrophy. No more locked and stuck in sin. It is time to move and exercise His power and His liberty.

Can the principles of physical rehabilitation and Story break through our spiritual scar tissue? Not by themselves. But they can point to the love of the Author of our Story, who heals and breaks through our wounds and scar tissue.

Story reveals vision, and vision reveals Story. If you know the Author and His Story, then you can have His vision for life, and as you have His vision for life, then you will see His Story more clearly. This truth is from your Author, who breaks the power of sin and its effects, and can heal you of your soul and spirit wounds. You are free to move toward your healing and your God. You have renewed strength emanating from God within you.

This is life-story rehab. Or perhaps even more accurately, this is life-story transformation in the hands of the Author.

Why are you still alive?

What do you live for?

Who do you live for?

What is *most important* in life?

I believe that if Jesus spoke to you through this book, He might say the following to you:

> *There were plots against your ancestors and against you in ways that you are aware of and in many more ways that you do not know. I stopped them. You are alive today because I desired you to be alive.*
>
> *Confess your sins. Even that one. Repent. Ask for my forgiveness. I forgive. Love me. Love others. Forgive others. Ask me to rule and reign within you.*
>
> *I am what you live for, and I desire to move within you to then move in the full liberty of walking with me in my strength and power flowing through you. I am in you, and you shall live for me. I am who you live for. Follow me. Walk with me above all others. I will show you how to move in the full liberty of movement and power that I have given you, and break the old scars that hold you back from ways I created unique to only you. Read my Story. Follow my ways. Go to my church. Love my people. I will show you how to navigate and flourish in the coming difficult days that no one has seen before.*
>
> *I have given you a new name, for you are mine. You are a new creature. Walk with me in newfound strength, and I will guide you to what is most important.*
>
> *When the prince of this world, with disappearing days, distracts you, fix your eyes on me and I will show you me through your new vision.*
>
> *I am the Author and perfecter of your faith.*
>
> *I am always with you.*

The Four Questions of the Apocalypse

- *Why* are you alive?
- *What* do you live for?
- *Who* do you live for?
- What is *most important* in life?

It Always Comes Back to Story

THE MOVEMENT AND STRENGTH ANALYSIS

CREATION   LOVE   CREATOR

What is Most Important in Life?

Creator in Me (SOAP Note)

Savior

Story

Student

Self

The Four Questions of the Apocalypse

You

SOAP NOTE

Subjective evidence
Objective evidence
Assessment
Plan

A Few of My Influences and Sources of Inspiration

"Mom Finds Kidnapped Daughter Six Years Later." CNN.com, March 2, 2004. https://www.cnn.com/2004/US/Northeast/03/01/girl.found.alive/.

Longley, Kyle. *The Morenci Marines: A Tale of Small Town America and the Vietnam War*. University Press of Kansas, 2013.

Heeren, Fred. *Show Me God: What the Message From Space Is Telling Us About God*. Searchlight Publications, 1995.

Ross, Hugh. *The Genesis Question: Scientific Advances and the Accuracy of Genesis*. NavPress, 1998.

Wurmbrand, Richard. *Tortured for Christ*. Living Sacrifice Book Company, 1998.

Johnson, Phillip E. *Defeating Darwinism by Opening Minds*. InterVarsity Press, 1997.

McDowell, Josh. *Evidence That Demands a Verdict: Historical Evidences for the Christian Faith, Volume 1*. Thomas Nelson Publishers, 1979.

New American Standard Bible, Thomas Nelson, Publishers 1976.